AN OPTIMIST'S BREXIT

A Millennial's Vision

Louis Williams

CONTENTS

A Step into the Great Unknown 3
Chapter 1: Getting the Best Deal with the EU 8
Chapter 2: Building the Great Meritocracy 18
Chapter 3: Forging an Open Trading World 25
Chapter 4: Crushing Crony Capitalism 30
Chapter 5: Building Bridges to a Brighter Future 35
Chapter 6: A Simple Selection of Charts 43
Chapter 7: Immigration, Integration and Innovation 47
Chapter 8: Green, Lean & Mean Manufacturing 54
Chapter 9: Financial Revolution 59
Chapter 10: True Tax Reform 68
Chapter 11: Welcome to the Age of Innovation 74
Chapter 12: Agricultural Awakening 79
Chapter 13: Antibureaucratic Planning 82
The End: Your Role in Building A Truly Great Britain 87
Economic Projections & Theory 89

A STEP INTO THE GREAT UNKNOWN

On the 24th of June 2016, I awoke to an election result almost no-one had anticipated. The United Kingdom had voted to leave the European Union. Under the stress and strain of the refugee migrant crisis on Europe's southern borders and buffeted by the winds of globalisation, the people of Britain voted to leave the political union which many had credited with maintaining peace & prosperity across Europe. Overnight the political map had been completely redrawn.

For many across the country, particularly my millennial generation, this was not just an act of economic suicide, but an abandonment of the fundamental liberal, open values that we hold so dear. European workers across the country awoke, not just angry about the result, but fearful of the consequences for their everyday lives. Would they be allowed to stay in this great country that they now call home? Car manufacturers across the North East began to realize that their whole supply chain across Europe could be broken by our withdrawal from the Customs Union.

However, for the majority of the country this was the day that the sun rose on a newly independent Britain. This was the opportunity to take back control of our borders, our laws and our money. As an £8.6bn net contributor to the EU, we would have this great Brexit dividend which could be invested in the NHS, Schools or other austerity hit public services. Libertarian Globalists such as Boris Johnson, Liam Fox and David Davis saw this as the chance to go out and rebuild our Commonwealth trade links and connect with the rest of the world. As Europe fades into economic insignificance it becomes vital for the UK to connect to the new hubs of prosperity across the globe.

I will admit to all those reading that, unlike many of my millennial cohort, I voted to Leave the European Union. I am the son of a Danish migrant, well-educated and a supposed "winner" from Globalisation. However, nonetheless on balance I saw the opportunities outside the EU as greater for the people of Britain than staying inside the EU. To me the EU was like a strait jacket, while it protects us from our worst nativist, protectionist instincts, it prevents us reaching our full potential by suffocating British industry with Franco-German regulation and prevents us confronting the issues of agricultural overcapacity.

For this reason, Brexit could lead to the economic reawakening of this great country or it could be the final stage of decline from our once great nation. In my book I hope to lay out a plan of how we can truly transform this country to make a Brexit that works for everyone and to build a Greater Britain together.

Why are we a nation in denial?

We are one of the wealthiest and most successful nations on the planet. Our universities have educated more world leaders than any other, we are the 2nd biggest aid donor globally and have the 5th largest economy in the globe.

People often talk about how we used to be great. How we used to command an empire and how we used to be the mightiest military in the world! People then almost seem to deify the great wartime leadership of Churchill, the state building prowess of Atlee and the transformational economics of Thatcher. People forget the great flaws of each respective chapter of history. How Churchill utterly mismanaged the UK as Chancellor in the 1920s when he oversaw Britain's disastrous return to the Gold Standard, which resulted in deflation, unemployment, and led to the General Strike of 1926. How Atlee's retreat from the world to finance the creation of the welfare state resulted in the secession of Pakistan and Bangladesh from India, precipitating many of the regional issues we see in South Asia today. Finally, how Thatcher's monetarism and the corresponding hike of interest rates crippled British manufacturing, even if her other reforms laid the foundations for the next 2 decades of prosperity.

People forget how much we have achieved in this period of relative decline. Even in manufacturing we are still the 6th largest manufacturer in the world. London is the financial capital of not just Europe, but also the Middle East and Africa. For all the talk of Chinese expansionism, the UK is still the largest source of foreign direct investment into Africa. Life expectancy has soared from 72.1 to 80.9 over the last 4 decades. More people are employed today in Britain than ever before, and no, this is not just immigrant labour boosting employment figures. Despite much scaremongering, only

13% of the British population was born abroad. These are British jobs for British workers.

On almost every metric you can think of, Brits alive today live longer, healthier and wealthier lives than their parents. While we have remained a dominant economic force in the world, we have receded from our past position of global leadership. Yet, we remain one of the only nations on earth capable of projecting force into any theatre of war across the globe. We will never again attain the global hegemony which we achieved in the heyday of the British empire, nevertheless the United Kingdom can and still is a global force for good.

However, for those who see Britain in a state of perpetual decline, Brexit is the final nail in the coffin of British soft power. Even if you take the stance that Britain has been in perpetual decline since the start of the 20th century, this need not be the final epitaph. In fact, I passionately believe that Brexit could be the catalyst that revives British soft power globally. Pivoting our focus from inward looking debates about Fortress Europe to how we can open up and access as many markets as possible globally. Along with likeminded globalist nations, such as Canada, Australia and New Zealand, we can forge a new free trading global order.

Since the 19th century Britain has been the bank of the world, even today 41% of global foreign exchange trading happens in the UK. English contract law is used for most international contracts across the globe, as the history and reputation of our legal and judicial system is second to none. Weak legal systems are one of the largest impediments for growth in middle income countries, such as India and China. Just take a moment to consider how large an economic boom could be realised if English contract law became recognisable and enforceable in China and India's domestic markets.

While the recent poor election result for the Conservatives and the prospect of a Corbynista socialist government has left even passionate Brexiteers questioning whether Brexit can still be a success, there is much reason for hope.

Uniting a divided nation

Along with 52% of our great nation, I chose to vote to leave the European Union. We reasoned that the European Union was holding back progress in the United Kingdom and diminishing our overall prosperity. However, 48% of our compatriots did not see the same way and this is not because they are a bunch of nervous, unpatriotic people willing to accept decline; they genuinely believed, with many valid reasons and arguments, that our future was brighter as part of the European Union.

The divides emerging today between the passionate Brexiteers, alt-left hardliners and metropolitan Remainers are threatening to undermine the cohesive society built over the past few decades. Politicians today receive countless death threats from both far right and increasingly far left activists. Sadly, over the past year since the referendum we have seen the continued growth of US style "shock jock" hyper partisanship, which has disabled US politics since the Obama era.

These divides will not be easy to cure, but it is fundamental that we, the Brexiteers, take the first step to bridge this divide. We have won the referendum and now we must show humility to those who have lost, not accuse them of being unpatriotic. Squabbling will only worsen the deal that we will get from the EU, so we must quickly come to a compromise on objectives with the Remain faction. We are a liberal democracy and that means taking into account the views and interests of the minorities, not an Erdogan/Putin style majoritarian dictatorship.

Many Remainers wanted to remain in the European Union because they wanted to have the opportunity to work, study and travel across Europe. Of course, if we are to regain control of our borders these freedoms will be curtailed on the European side, we can't demand protection of our labour market and assume borderless access to Europe. However, there appears to be little appetite on either side to close off cross border studying and travel opportunities. We should offer the Remainers the clear objective of visa free study and holidaying throughout the European Union, along with continued participation in the Erasmus program.

Beyond the movement of people, the objectives of Remainers and Brexiteers don't appear to be significantly at odds. Both groups want to achieve frictionless or near frictionless trade with the EU. And although in order to properly leave the EU it is essential to leave the single market, it is possible, as in Switzerland, to retain most of the current access rights outside of the single market.

Sadly, however, curing the divisions within the UK will take longer than the 2 years of Brexit negotiations. Whatever deal we come to, will leave many factions unsatisfied, because every deal requires compromise. However, reaching that compromise will be the first step that pulls us closer together from the polarised political climate we have enveloped ourselves in. Where every piece of good economic news released, is "proof" that Brexit will do no harm, while every stumbling block & challenge in the negotiations is seized on to say that the talks are doomed to failure. Frankly, this naked partisanship on both sides is a self-defeating malaise, which may develop into the hyper partisanship that we see across the pond in America.

Rather than focusing on our divisions, we should focus on what unites us. We may have disagreements over exactly how the NHS should be structured and exactly how much money should be diverted from Education or Defence to finance it. However, almost everybody believes that we should have universal healthcare. We may not like unilateral interventionism, but we agree that UN missions should include British soldiers. And we all agree that there is a problem in regard to housing, that we need to build more, but struggle when it gets to the how. These disagreements are so minimal in relation to the divisions we see in this world, even with the hard left taking control of the Labour movement, Labour's policy proposals aren't exactly hard left.

The government must take the first step of trying to build unity, by trying to table a cross party policy agenda on a shared cause with co-sponsorship from both Labour and the Liberal Democrats. How about proposing a national infrastructure plan where MPs of every region come together to propose infrastructure development plans for their local areas? What if regional MPs of all parties join together to work on the challenges facing the NHS, schools and the police in their local area? Imagine for a minute that if we worked collectively we could ensure that no military veterans are left homeless on the streets of this country. This country needs to be brought back together and start the process of becoming united again, under common goals and a common vision of a Greater Britain. Then we can move onto the complicated challenge of achieving the Best Deal for Britain.

CHAPTER 1: GETTING THE BEST DEAL WITH THE EU

Today 61% of our trade is either with the EU or with a country who the EU has trade agreements with. To fall out of the EU with no trade agreement would be cataclysmic for the economy, wages and jobs. Falling back onto a WTO agreement would cripple auto production, pharmaceuticals and high-tech manufacturing in this country. For services, the consequences would be far less severe, as there is no true single market in services in the European Union. Nonetheless we need a credible plan in the event of failure in these negotiations.

Many people know the old adage that if you fail to plan, you plan to fail. In the case of negotiations, if you plan for failure, you massively boost your chance of success.

To elaborate, I will use the example of Greece and Syriza's failed negotiations with the Troika. Yanis Varafoukis, a well-educated economics professor, decided to use his expertise in Game Theory to outwit and play the Troika. Yanis knew that Greece had no credible means to threaten the EU; to unilaterally drop out of the Euro and leave the European Union would mean abandoning the regional development subsidies, one of the most important sources of investment in the Greek economy. Therefore, he tried to play the "madman", he tried to convince the Troika that he was genuinely willing to pull Greece out of the Euro and European Union if he didn't get enough debt forgiveness from the Troika. Unfortunately, the straight-laced Troika, just saw this as folly and did not buckle to his demands; without a credible threat, he had to take whatever he was offered.

This is why David Davis is right to say we must be prepared to walk away if we are offered a bad deal. No deal must be better than a bad deal.

So, what would a credible "no deal plan" look like?

Well the no deal plan must satisfy 2 clear criteria:

1. It must be economically beneficial for the UK, or at least good enough that it would be an acceptable outcome.
2. It must be significantly damaging to the EU, so that they see the true cost of refusing to negotiate in good faith.

Welcome to the concept of the Singapore West model. The EU is terrified by the prospect of a tax haven on or near their near border, particularly with footloose tech companies able to locate anywhere largely unaffected by trade barriers and other protectionist measures.

Rolling back regulatory red tape, abolishing air passenger duty & cutting corporation tax to 5% for all companies domiciled in the UK would lead to mass offshoring of professional services, financial services and technology firms. Introducing a new streamlined process for skilled migrant hires would remove any fears about access to talent in a newly independent Britain. This sort of model would cause a collapse in investment levels across the remainder of EU and deprive EU governments of much needed tax revenue. However, for the UK the divisions of the country would grow even wider, as London and the prosperous South East see a surge of inward investment, while the Midlands and North-East experience the second great deindustrialisation as newly imposed EU customs duties collapse Pan-European supply chains. Nonetheless, this would appear as a credible no deal plan for the UK to present in negotiations, if necessary.

Having established a credible back stop plan, we should now look to what we want to change post Brexit:

1. Control of our borders
2. Control of our laws (social, economic, environmental)
3. Ability to sign free trade deals with other nations
4. Pay less into the EU

And what we hope to keep post Brexit:

1. Full access to the single market
2. Customs free access to EU market
3. Pan-European study opportunities

4. Participation in Pan-European Research Programs
5. Visa free tourist access
6. British Citizens rights in Europe

Now of course it would be lovely to think that we could just achieve all of the above without compromise, however, we can't just have our cake and eat it. But we can get pretty close, if we begin to think what the EU wants:

1. Minimal disruption to trade
2. Ability to sell this deal as worse than EU membership
3. No change to the 4 fundamental freedoms of the single market
4. European Citizens rights in the UK
5. Net financial contributions from the UK

Initially these objectives may seem completely incompatible with the goals of the British negotiators. After al,l if we take back control of our borders and kept access to the single market, surely we would be violating the 4 fundamental freedoms of the single market?

Actually, no.

We cannot stay in the single market in order to satisfy the "red lines" of both sides, however there is nothing whatsoever preventing some form of comprehensive market access agreement. But I will get back to that later, first off, I'd like to introduce you to the core constituent parts of the European Union. Unfortunately, the next bit is going to get quite technical so bear with me.

ECU vs EEA vs EFTA (European Customs Union vs Single Market vs European Free Trade Association)

The European Customs Union was first formed in 1968 to create a region where all goods could move without any tariff or customs charge. Underpinning this free movement of goods is the Common External Tariff, a rule whereby any good which enters the ECU is charged a fixed tariff regardless of how it entered. So it didn't matter if say steel was imported into Holland or Denmark, they would be charged the same tariff upon entry. This ensures that no country can undercut another, as a cheap entry point into Europe. However, if the steel was produced and made from iron and coal within the ECU it would face no tariff whatsoever and would be free to move from Aberystwyth to Gdansk with no impediment. All members of the EU are members of the ECU; however, they are also joined by Turkey, Andorra and Monaco.

So, hang on isn't that the single market?

Again, no.

The single market or European Economic Area, is a region with harmonised regulations across goods and some services. This means that they meet the same product standards wherever they are sold in the EEA. This removes what we call non-tariff barriers to trade or in layman's terminology rules that block the trade and sale of foreign goods. For instance, before the formation of the single market, France could require that for every car sold in France 75% of the parts had to be made in France. This would effectively ban all foreign cars from being sold in the French market. Being part of the EEA, means that no country can treat cars manufactured within any other EEA country differently to cars manufactured within the UK.

The single market has 2 further "freedoms", labour & capital. Freedom of movement of labour means simply that every EEA citizen has the right to live and work in any other EEA nation and be treated the same as a native. This is one of the most contentious issues to the British and any settlement where this remains could be very tricky for the British to accept. In contrast, free movement of capital is possibly the least contentious issue, with most nations accepting that the free movement of capital across borders is highly beneficial in most scenarios. Codifying free movement of capital could protect us from the whims of a radicalist left or Trumpist right, who might seek in the future to implement ludicrously damaging capital controls.

In addition, the single market has evolved to include the regulation of environmental policy, judging, quite reasonably, that harmonised environmental regulation will prevent countries undercutting each other to boost industrial competitiveness.

Finally, we reach the final core agreement, the European Free Trade Agreement. Don't worry we're almost there.

The European Free Trade Association simply means that all goods which are at least 90% produced within an EFTA nation can be sold to any other EFTA nation without facing a tariff. If a nation is within the ECU, this is automatically assumed, as otherwise the good would have already been charged the common external tariff. However, for nations inside EFTA and outside the ECU, they must prove the origin of the goods sold to other EFTA nations, which can be particularly burdensome when you consider how long and complex some supply chains are.

Other than that, there are a multitude of shared programs run by the EU: research (Horizon), agricultural & fisheries policies (CAP & CFP), education (Erasmus), labour rights (social chapter) & regional development funds administered by EU officials. Despite these programs being peripheral to the core trade deals, these are programs that the EU wants continued funding for.

There we are, we're done. If you need a refresh, just check the Recap below, otherwise please move on and let's get on to the interesting part. The negotiation.

Recap

ECU (European Customs Union):

1. No taxes on goods traded across borders within the ECU
2. Standardised tax on goods sold into the ECU from outside

EEA (European Economic Area, aka the "Single Market"):

1. Freedom of movement of goods
2. Freedom of movement of services (although only some services)
3. Freedom of movement of labour
4. Freedom of movement of capital
5. EEA wide identical regulations (environment, goods, services, labour & capital)
6. Gold plating/extra regulation allowed in countries (environment, services & labour)

EFTA (European Free Trade Association):

1. Tax free trade of EFTA countries goods across borders within EFTA
2. If outside of ECU, need to prove origin of goods to prevent countries evading the Common External Tariff

The negotiation

Negotiations are always iterative. So, the structure of the negotiation affects the shape of the final deal and therefore whoever sets the structure of the negotiations will gain the upper hand. The EU have already done this by announcing that no negotiation on the future trade deal was possible until our outstanding financial obligations or "Brexit Bill" is agreed and the rights of EU citizens in Britain is accepted.

The least painful issue in this negotiation is citizens' rights. Both sides seem willing to agree to a reciprocal deal on citizens' rights. Concluding this with speed will win some early goodwill with our EU allies, while conveniently boosting economic confidence among migrants already present in the UK.

Unfortunately, the negotiation about the "Brexit Bill" is likely to be contentious and tricky, therefore in response to the EU's demands it is vital that we strengthen our hand to temper the excessive demands of the EU.

Strengthening our hand

The reality is that the EU represents an economic block 5 times larger than the UK individually. The damage of a collapse in trade would be more severe for the UK than for the EU. Therefore, it is vital alongside the "Singapore West" model detailed above, that the UK prepares the mother of all stimulus efforts to let the UK economy ride over the uncertainty. Fortunately, the Treasury has already prepared the ground for this by pushing back the deadline for a balanced budget to 2022. So, with so much uncertainty over tariffs, regulation and market access, how on Earth can the UK government provide companies certainty?

Through 3 simple policies:

1. Guarantee to pay all ECU tariffs for UK exporters until 2022 if we are forced into trading on WTO rules
2. Match all EU research funding for UK projects unconditionally until 2025
3. Announce a new regional infrastructure fund equal to the current EU regional aid budget available until 2025

This simple set of policies would cost the treasury at most £7.6bn annually for 6 years. However, the great thing about these policies is that they will, likely, never have to be implemented and combined with the threat of a "Singapore West" plan, they would push the EU back to the negotiating table.

Vitally these plans should be published to the British people. By publicly declaring the plan for a "no deal" Brexit, the threat would become credible, not just a neo liberals pipe dream. In response to the predicted outpouring of criticism from European leaders and the UK left and threats of UK financial services being banned from operating anywhere in the EEA. The government can simply respond that "We have no wish to implement these plans and hope to work with the EU constructively to find a plan which suits both sides, but it would be both irresponsible and foolish to not plan for such an outcome. Furthermore, we only make this public announcement in response to the EU's request for openness, this is no threat merely our openness."

Simultaneously the UK government can blunt the threat of a left-wing rebellion by announcing a series of relaxations to fiscal policy for ordinary working people. For instance, announcing the provision of free school breakfasts for every child across the country would be a relatively inexpensive way of announcing to the people that the government was on the side of working families.

Onto the back foot

The EU has made a core assumption after the election that the UK government is fatally weakened by the recent election and that the threat of a Corbyn government will force the UK to play a safe game. Throwing caution to the wind with such an announcement will completely wrong foot the EU negotiators, while boosting investor and consumer confidence across the UK.

The UK can then deliver its opening gambit on the "Brexit Bill", we can agree to every pound of expenditure up to 2019 and the continued financing of the programs we wish to partake in: i.e. Horizon, Erasmus and EHIC. Simultaneously, we refuse to pay a penny towards the regional development fund, European institutional costs, the Common Agricultural Policy and the Common Fisheries Policy which combined make up 70% of the cost of EU membership.

The EU will certainly refuse this opening offer and respond that unless we improve our offer there will be no trade deal, no access. Thanks to the tariff guarantees announced by the UK government, UK investor confidence will shudder but face no collapse. Meanwhile, business confidence across Europe will begin to wane as the threat of tax competition from a Singapore West on Europe's borders becomes an increasingly realistic prospect. Splits will begin to emerge as Eastern European members argue with French farmers and Northern European net contributors about where the missing €10bn of UK net contributions will come from.

After a few months of brinkmanship, the UK should then offer a goodwill gesture to continue financing the regional development fund until the next European funding round. After the addition of a couple of additional sweeteners, it is entirely reasonable to believe that the EU will accept the deal as an attempt to shore up divisions among the constituent parties about who will pay for the bill.

But what about the "Brexit Bill" agreed with the EU already in the December round of negotiations? Surely that would sink any hope of playing hardball with the EU and achieving all of the above! Haven't we already agreed to pay them for leaving? Not really. No. At the moment, all we have suggested is that we will!

Planning for the future

The UK should not try and stay in the single market. It would be impossible to regain control of our laws or borders under this scenario and would basically result in us being ruled under dictat from Brussels, certainly a worse option than just staying part of the club. Instead the UK should be unashamedly ambitious. Offering to leave the Customs Union and single market while remaining part of EFTA and gaining full access to the single market.

Initially, the EU will flat out refuse the demands, accusing the UK of cherry picking and being completely mad. The UK at this point should not budge an inch and simply say that we are offering a fair trade of full access to each other's markets, a continued partnership built on joint prosperity. We don't want to be part of the political project of the EU, but we want to be incredibly close partners to ensure each other's prosperity. Exploiting the strategy described above, we can achieve a deal outside of both the Customs Union and the single market, but with extensive access and no continuing payments to EU institutions.

What about Northern Ireland and Gibraltar?

Northern Ireland and Gibraltar do present unique problems in regard to the final settlement that we will come to with the EU. Unfortunately, these two regions are far more tied into the economic fabric of the European Economic Area and are far more dependent on other European nations for their economic livelihoods. However, the solution for each will need to be different due to the reality that the European Union has stated that the final deal will not apply to Gibraltar, unless Spain acquiesces. Which, in light of the police state crackdown in Cataluña, seems increasingly unlikely. Nonetheless, I will first confront the issue of Northern Ireland and the "invisible border" with the Republic of Ireland.

Since the Good Friday agreement of 1998, we have had almost 20 years of peace in Northern Ireland. No civilised person wants to go back to the dark days of the troubles and Remainers are completely fair to raise objection to a "clean Brexit" over concerns for the peace of Northern Ireland. It would be abhorrent to me if my vote for independence from Europe led to the explosion of instability in Northern Ireland. However, how do we keep an invisible border in Northern Ireland, unless we remain within the Customs Union? There are 2 options to achieve this, either we sign a trade deal with the EU allowing for free movement of goods across borders or Northern Ireland has to stay within the Customs Union with an internal tariff border with the rest of the UK. The 2nd option would probably lead to a collapse in the government with the DUP withdrawing support or even more worryingly could flare up tensions between the unionists and republicans.

The reality is that the Ireland border issue cannot be resolved until we have some idea about the ending trade deal. Anything else suggested by the EU is absolute rubbish. The sole reason the EU have chosen to frontload this at the beginning of the negotiation is to try and force the UK to stay in the single market and customs union in all but name. The negotiators rather cunningly have tried to trap the Brexit negotiating team into a position where any deal which doesn't threaten the peace in Northern Ireland, requires the UK to stay in the single market. The UK wisely refused to come to a "hard" deal on Northern Ireland before we have got on to trade talks and the EU accepted a "soft" indication of intent. If the EU insists again on an agreement about the border prior to conclusion of trade talks, we need to be ready to walk away from the negotiations and start piling the pressure on the EU. Unfortunately, sometimes a show of strength is the only way to make the other side understand we are being serious.

The case of Gibraltar is possibly a little simpler. Gibraltar overwhelmingly voted to stay in the EU with 96% of voters voting to Remain and in addition we need Spain's approval for the eventual deal for the UK to apply to Gibraltar. In light of these two dominant factors and how integrated Gibraltar is within the European Economic Area, we should look for a solution with Spain where Gibraltar remains part of the Single Market and Customs Union. Gibraltar, unlike the rest of the UK, is too dependent on trade with Spain to thrive outside of Europe. However, Gibraltar is a unique case in this regard. Pragmatism is the British way.

The Final Deal?

Now these negotiating steps laid out above should help the UK government take steps towards achieving a better deal for Britain. Yet nothing is ever guaranteed. The eventual deal will probably end up being settled only a month or so before the UK "crashes out" of Europe, as brinkmanship dominates these political negotiations. This will unfortunately lead to some slowing of the UK economy, as businesses put off investment decisions. Even with the economic stabilisers suggested above, growth will be tepid for the next year and a half as uncertainty over the deal hangs over the UK economy. However, once this uncertainty lifts, the UK will witness a rapid surge in growth as postponed investments are pushed forward, creating jobs, wage growth and boosting tax revenues. Over the next few years, we are in for an economic ride, but we could easily end up with a fantastic final deal.

CHAPTER 2: BUILDING THE GREAT MERITOCRACY

"You can't have a competitive, egalitarian meritocracy if only some of your citizens have the opportunity for a good education." – Rupert Murdoch

Brexit presents the greatest opportunity for an economic and social revolution in Britain. For all the merits of the neoliberal revolution in the 1980s and the prosperity that it brought to the UK, an increase in social mobility was not one of them. As of today, children from foster care represent 27% of the prison population, workers educated in UK private schools earn 17% more than state school educated workers within 3 years of graduating and are 4 times more likely to be a millionaire. If we are to build a truly Great Britain we must exploit the skills of our entire population, not just the social elite.

People across the country despair at the prospect that their children will grow up with fewer life chances than themselves. Children from troubled backgrounds are told that their results "are good considering your situation", while families with means pay for hundreds of extra hours every year with external tutors. Meanwhile, we grant increased benefits to the baby boomer generation at the expense of investment in education and financial support for parents. Inheritance or parental support is seen as the only option for many to get on the housing ladder, further widening the gulf of opportunity between those from wealthy backgrounds and regular households.

It does not have to be this way. The solution is not more money but a new prioritisation of resources. Education is the great leveller, it equips children with the skills which will enable them to compete in this newly globalised world. Education is a weapon of social reform, it allows us to correct for the existence of ill equipped parents, schools can be a substitute for aspects of parenting. Children do not just require education and skills, they require guidance.

I remember a simple conversation I had with my parents when I was deciding what A-levels to pick which went something like this:

Me: "What do you think I should pick for my A-Levels?"
Parents: "Well that's hard to say. What do you enjoy most at school?"
Me: "Ooh. Umm. Maths, Science, Drama and Sport, but I probably enjoy Drama a little more."
Parents: "What do you want to do after studying?"

That last question was the most important question. Too often children are told just to study what they enjoy most, ignoring the doors it opens and closes for their future. By going through the different opportunities available to me after studying each subject I came to the simple conclusion that I should focus on my maths and science and could still do drama on the side for fun. Too many children finish school and realise too late that they don't have the skills which employers need. Every year we hear that there aren't enough STEM and language graduates and that ordinary Brits numeric and computing skills are insufficient for the needs of our modern-day economy.

Middle class kids have access to a multitude of language exchanges, extra tutoring and music lessons. They receive continual guidance from parents about what opportunities exist and what are the consequences of their decisions. In reality, education spreads well beyond the school environment, however, few governments have truly recognised the significance of "out of school learning". More than that, "out of school learning" has been seen as a nice added extra, which is a luxury for the wealthy rather than a fundamental component of the education system.

Falling Through the Gaps

Despite negativity in much of the old stream press, educational outcomes across Britain have risen not fallen over the last couple of decades. However, the attainment gap between those from wealthy backgrounds and ordinary schoolkids has widened. The average child in private education today is twice as likely to get an A or an A* at A level and has a 800% higher chance of being admitted into Oxbridge.

The answer proposed by the radical left has been to close the private schooling system and ban private tutoring to level the playing field. This is just utterly barmy. We would be saying to people, if you're rich don't do the responsible thing and invest in your child's education, just waste all your cash on fancier holidays, a bigger house and a car. In fact, we can learn a lot from the success story of the private schooling system of the UK.

Girls at single sex private schools are 75% more likely to study Maths at A-Level than those outside of the private school system. Private school students do 3.4 hours more sport a week and girls are encouraged to pursue their academic strengths regardless of the gender stereotypes that may exist. Pupils at private school do over an hour more musical practice, travel to twice as many countries on educational trips and are twice as likely to be involved in a language exchange.

While private schools continue to produce students with the skills for the modern economy, the public schooling system has failed to keep up with the needs of industry. We have a skills deficit or more precisely a "relevant skills deficit". Kids today are better educated than ever before, but are studying the wrong skills. This has resulted in the depressing outcome for many graduates who leave university with raised expectations disappointed that they cannot find any "graduate level jobs". Industry needs armies of STEM and languages to deal with the hi tech multi lingual business world, while our education system churns out legions of social science and humanity graduates. Equally firms require mechanics and those with a technical understanding of machinery to work in our highly automated factories.

Time and time again industry bodies tell us their needs, and nothing is done. Imagine if we built a system where every child was programming literate, numerical and multilingual. Supported by the best universities in the world, the next Facebook or Google would not be founded in the US, but in the UK, which could be the future technological powerhouse of the world.

If this seems far-fetched, just consider the ecosystem which already exists in the UK. Flexible labour markets, world leading universities, deep venture capital pools, low corporate taxes and one of the simplest systems of company formation and reporting in the world. If we turn our schooling system into the envy of the world, no other nation will rival the UK for leadership in the high technology space.

Education 2020

The first step to building a fairer society is education.

If the UK is to forge ahead as a global leader, it will need to revolutionise it's approach to learning by adopting the best aspects of both foreign educational systems and our own highly successful private schooling system. Educational reform does not need an explosion of spending but a refocussing of resources, around the needs of a 21st century society.

"Information is power" and education is the best way to spread that information to every child in the country.

Providing the Basic Skills

Over the 20th century we managed to attain 99.9% academic literacy and numeracy. Almost every adult and child can read and write and, although many are numerically weak for the needs of many of their jobs, they are capable of functioning in everyday life. This is in retrospect a fantastic and vital achievement of developed countries across the globe. However, these skills are not sufficient for the basic jobs of the future. Computer and programming literacy will soon become a prerequisite of the job market which our children will enter into. Equally we live in a far more globalised world than that of our parents and if we wish to make the most of Brexit, it is vital that our children are able to speak the languages of the world (Mandarin, Spanish, Arabic & Russian).

Schools in their traditional form are particularly poorly designed to teach both programming and languages. Immersion in both computer and natural languages has been shown to considerably outperform "spread out" classroom teaching. Put simply immersion works. Immersion, particularly in natural languages has a secondary benefit of boosting cultural understanding alongside equipping children with the linguistic skills they require. Further this is a tried and tested method both for programming and language education.

Intensive programming colleges are popping up across the world offering 3-6 month immersion courses, as people choose to invest in their own future, recognising the inadequacy of school teaching of the subject. Under immersion it is possible to become competent in 3 programming languages within 6 months. Equally it only takes 3 months of immersion for the average Latin-based language student to reach A level standard.

People may suggest that all of the above may be well and good, but that an immersion program is something we cannot afford. I would suggest that we cannot afford not to do it. If we want to remain ahead of the pack, we must recognise that the UK must become the number 1 destination for international businesses to locate and this means not just low taxes and business friendly regulation, but the skilled workforce they need.

In addition, due to the relatively high cost of living in the UK an international immersion program could be cheaper than a year of education in the UK. As an example, an 11-month Mandarin Immersion program in mainland China with 20 hours of lessons a week, shared apartments and a £150/month living stipend and return flights to London would cost around £5900 in total, almost identical to a year of schooling back home, despite all living costs being covered out in China.

Immersive computing courses are also relatively inexpensive with a year of programming education costing £5500.

The government should offer students the opportunity to spend a year becoming immersed in languages overseas or immersed in a programming education. They could be empowered to either take this year directly after completing their GCSEs or the year after they complete their A-levels/technical college. Students and parents would be empowered to take the decision of whether they wanted that year out of conventional education or just to continue with their core studies.

This immersion year would be a weapon of social mobility. Enabling every child to have the skills to compete in the modern era. For those "exchanging" to developing nations overseas, they would be exposed to some of the harsher realities of the world. They would also build connections which could very well become our trading relationships of the future. The combination of linguistic skills, cultural immersion and these international contacts would open vast opportunities for the hundreds of thousands of students leaving education every year.

The immersion year would show that Brexit was about the UK opening up to the world not closing the door on Europe.

Educational Technology Revolution

Reform, however, must step far beyond filling the basic skill gaps that exist in the UK educational system. It must also be about transporting our educational system into the 21st century, embracing the leading teaching techniques both inside and outside the classroom.

Today it is possible to enrol online into a university lecture series with notes, tests and class feedback for free. Instead of paying £9,000 for a year of undergraduate lectures in a second-tier university of the UK, you can access lectures by world class academics at the best institutions straight to your laptop. Massive Online Open Courses (MOOCs for short) are the first stage of an educational revolution, where a quality education becomes cheap and accessible to all with a high school education. The next generation of online tools will be educational applications, games and courses accessible to children with little or no academic knowledge or training.

How fast Educational Technology takes holds, depends on the flexibility and forward thinking of government. For too long government resources have focussed on the insider, funnelling public money through established schools and local education authorities, while ignoring the ground-breaking potential of educational technology and private educational tutoring and classes. The government has already recognised that central control has failed in education and so embracing the creed of decentralisation could ensure that our educational system becomes a world leader on all fronts. It is time to go beyond the Academisation program and bring educational reform to the next level; through Academisation we have already pushed down funding and teaching decisions from the centre to the schools. Let us take this one step further and push spending power down to the parents. Give parents educational vouchers which could be spent on schooling, private tuition or educational technology.

Schools would be able to charge equal to or less than the value of the educational vouchers and parents would be free to spend any surplus educational vouchers on external tuition, music lessons or educational technologies. Suddenly working-class kids would have the opportunity to access resources previously reserved for the affluent middle class. On top of this, the mind set of investing in your children's education beyond the classroom would become entrenched among families across the country. This reform would allow schools to innovate to deliver teaching at a lower cost, rather than maximising spending within a budget.

The immersion year could also become part of this, with parents allocated educational vouchers to spend on a combination of language immersion, programming courses alongside educational technologies etc. Parents and their children could collectively decide which program to enrol in, instead of being compelled by the state to select a particular program. This would have the added benefit of engaging parents and students in the educational process, acutely aware of how much this year of education was costing.

These reforms would take years not months to bear fruit, but would over time lay the building blocks for a prosperous post Brexit future. However, it is possible in our lifetime that the United Kingdom will emerge as the academic and technological leader of this world. We need not the largest army, nor the largest population to shape this world and our future, but the brightest and most technologically capable population of the world.

CHAPTER 3: FORGING AN OPEN TRADING WORLD

"Globalism began as a vision of a world with free trade, shared prosperity, and open borders. These are good, even noble things to aim for." – Deepak Chopra

In 1756, Adam Smith wrote that the Wealth of a Nation was built not on the resource superiority of a nation, but their ability to exploit their comparative advantages through trade and commerce to enrich our world in comparison to our Autarkic forbearers. International trade and commerce has not only helped create previously unimaginable wealth in economically advanced nations, but also lifted billions out of poverty. In the last 3 decades 500mn Chinese have been lifted out of poverty thanks to their opening up to internal and international trade. Free trade has created complex global supply chains, where the cotton in the American designed jeans I wear is grown in India, weaved in Bangladesh, tied together with thread from Ethiopia, combined with a zip manufactured in China using ores from Australia, before being treated and coloured in Italy before being sold to me in a store in Britain.

Free trade and globalisation is continually attacked as the exploitation of the world by faceless multinationals, forcing down environmental standards and imposing colonial style control on developing nations. This is frankly rubbish, well strictly, the criticism of free trade in this particular light is. Large corporations have exploited consumers in both developing and developed countries, exploiting regulatory loopholes and lobbyist connections to rig the system in their favour. For those angry at the exploitation of multinationals, do not turn your anger towards free trade, but instead this crony capitalism, which I offer some solutions to in step 4.

Free trade and competition do not enrich large corporations, but instead forces down prices and squeezes their profit margins. Free trade is the weapon through which we can make sure that companies work for their consumers, not to exploit them. Free trade enables us to reject the firm who exploits us and choose from any of the other firms operating in this world. With protectionist populists across the world from the USA to Greece emboldened, the need to fight for a free trading world is more relevant than ever.

Some commentators have tried to group the Brexit rebellion in the same basket as the rise of Trump, Geert Wilders or Marine Le Pen. This is ultimately fallacious. Many who voted to leave the EU, did not do it to close the door on Europe, but rather open our drawbridge to the rest of the world. The UK can and should take the lead in securing and expanding a new free trading world order. This means taking uncomfortable decisions, such as exposing our molly coddled agricultural sector to outside competition. I would be lying if I said the transition won't be painful, change always is. However, the opportunities of free trade vastly outweigh these growing pains.

Post Brexit Jump

Immediately after we leave the EU, it will be vital to secure quick free trade agreements to ensure that our companies gain the market access they need to prosper and expand into foreign markets. Now many commentators may say that there are no quick deals to be made post Brexit, however, I beg to differ. This is thanks to what can be called open platform trade deals. Effectively open platform trade deals allow any country to join, provided they accept the existing terms of the trade agreement and do not demand any adjustments.

This theoretically means that, the day after Brexit, the UK would be able to sign onto these open platform trade deals. Now, no deals are completely open, many in fact are only open to a select group of countries. However, there is no reason why the UK could not seek to be added to this list of countries prior to Brexit. The UK can technically not sign any trade deals until it leaves the EU, but it can receive pre-approval for entry!

In particular the Trans Pacific Partnership, offers the UK the opportunity for a quick win trade deal. At the moment, the trade agreement is only open to members of APEC and other nations which they approve. However, with some canny diplomatic efforts there would be no reason for the TPP to refuse the UK's application, as the UK is a developed economy offering a market worth over $2tn to TPP exporters.

The second, vital quick trade deal, would be with the US. Now you may instinctively think 2 things make this a "pie in the sky" dream. First off, the US has now elected a, seemingly, protectionist president with nationalist instincts, who fundamentally believes that his countries problems are down to the Chinese "raping" the American economy with their cheap exports. Secondly, bilateral deals take far too much time to give the UK a quick easy win post Brexit.

Well yes, strictly the 2 facts above are true. However, the deal maker in chief has already got stuck in the Washington swamp and he needs to show that he can sign a great deal. Secondly the UK need not sign a bilateral deal with the US, but could join an already existing agreement in the form of NAFTA. A trade deal with the UK through NAFTA could offer Trump a face saving way out of a damaging trade war with Mexico, while being able to claim a newly reformed "America First" NAFTA with the UK a new market for American exporters.

These two simple steps would not only give the British economy an economic jump start post Brexit, but also massively strengthen the UK's negotiating position with the EU.

Changing the Conversation

Shaping the post Brexit free trading world order will not be as quick or easy as our first potential deals with NAFTA and the TPP. These negotiations will be more complex and time consuming, yet the rewards of deeper more comprehensive trade deals will be vast. Many suggest that comprehensive trade deals are almost impossible, as each concession towards market access or open trade is a battle in itself. The default at the start of every negotiation is to continue as is, and each change is argued over and dispute.

The UK should radically depart from this negotiating style onto one where the assumption is complete openness and market access, where protections are then added for certain industries. By assuming that all trade will face no tariffs and mutually recognising each other's regulations, you change the whole debate. If we say to Australia that we assume that all goods and services that meet their standards meet ours and they treat us reciprocally, then every company will face no border whatsoever to operating across country borders.

Changing the conversation to "what has to be protected", rather than "what can we open up to competition" would radically reshape negotiations. Negotiating times would dramatically fall and the end deal would be far deeper and more comprehensive than under previous regimes. Yes, this would mean fighting off special interest groups and could be politically expensive in the short run. However, incompatible regulation is the biggest barrier to trade today, it limits competition and technological progress and leaves us all the poorer for it.

Imagine the opportunities if firms operating in mainland China could conduct business under English contract law without the uncertainty of China's politicised courts. Imagine if a neurosurgeon in Glasgow could conduct remote surgery in South Africa using a surgical robot and cameras, offering lifesaving treatment to someone unable to travel to the UK. Architects in Cardiff could design skyscrapers across Hong Kong remotely without any extra license, recognising that their expertise and certification in the UK was relevant anywhere in the world.

We should look to free trade as an opportunity to rejuvenate our most economically deprived areas and drive a renaissance. Industrial zones across the country should be reclassified as free ports where any input can be imported tariff free and re-exported to establish the UK into international supply chains. These tariff free zones would be used to create export jobs in zones such as Plymouth, Hull and Clydeside, which have seen industrial decline, but little to replace it.

These small free trade zones are particularly attractive for economically depressed areas, because they will have almost no de-industrialising effect on nearby areas, as there is little to no industry left to divert into the free port zones. With open trade and these free ports, any company choosing where to locate globally would see the UK as the gateway to the world. Free trade is not something to fear, but instead something to embrace.

False Trade-Offs: Jobs or Cheap Goods

Opening globally to trade will first require winning the argument at home, before we can forge ahead building a free trading world order. This will mean beating back the false narratives of protectionism, particularly closet protectionism. You will hear very respectable individuals start to talk about the need for a comprehensive trade strategy to ensure that:

1. Strategic industries are kept in the UK and supported to meet geopolitical needs.
2. Infant industrial sectors are nurtured by the UK government, so they can grow large enough to compete internationally.
3. That we should be willing to pay a little more for our consumer goods to protect jobs.

These ideas above seem sensible enough at initial glance. Doesn't it make intuitive sense that the government should seek to ensure that the UK agricultural sector is self sufficient to support ourselves in times of war and so we should dole out subsidies for the purpose of "economic security"? How on earth could the next start up Microsoft possibly hope to compete with the real Microsoft and other tech giants? So shouldn't the government step in to give a "helping hand"? Isn't paying £1 more for that t-shirt worth it so that more clothing manufacturing jobs are kept in the country?

No. No. And no.

1. The UK has not been agriculturally self-sufficient since 1800 and currently imports 41% of our food consumed. The UK with its tiny landmass will always struggle to be self-sufficient, so instead we should build a broad enough trade network, so we can switch between suppliers if we face a crisis.
2. Start-ups don't need protection, but as wide a market to access as possible to grow and develop. That means open free trade agreements and mutual regulatory recognition, not tariffs and subsidies. ARM developed into a £17bn business thanks to being open with the world not shutting it off. Protectionism stifles innovation, it does not foster entrepreneurial creation.
3. Protecting one sector diverts spending towards that sector and away from others. When you spend £1 more on that T-shirt, that's £1 less being spent in restaurants, cinemas etc. That means job losses in restaurants and the rest of the economy, while workers work in clothing factories ill-suited for their skill sets at lower real wages. Protectionism doesn't create jobs, it just replaces some jobs with other jobs and drives real wages down.

The only people who gain from protectionism are the privileged insiders, who see supernormal profits and higher wages at the expense of everybody else. Protectionism is like an anti-Robin Hood, government stealing from the poor and the weak and giving to the wealthy and powerful. Only through an open free trading Brexit can we bring prosperity to all in the UK, not just the protected insiders.

CHAPTER 4: CRUSHING CRONY CAPITALISM

If I told you that we currently have to abide by 13,450 EU binding acts and regulations every day, you would probably be shocked and amazed that there were so many laws governing our lives set by EU regulators under the single market. You'd probably wonder how many could be trimmed and you would be unsettled to learn that there has never been a year when the number of regulations has fallen. When will it stop, when does bureaucracy get too big?

In fact, all of the above is true, except that we have to abide by 134,500 EU regulations. Yes, 10 times the amount stated above. These diktats are part of the ever-sprawling leviathan of single market competencies. Although thousands of these rules are valid, useful and indeed necessary, tens of thousands exist purely due to the lobbying effects of big business and protected insider groups. These rules are not in the interest of consumers or the European public, but are instead carve-outs to allow firms to avoid competition and exploit consumers.

In Brussels, there are 30,000 people employed in lobbying to influence regulations in the favour of existing firms, trade unions and interest groups. This is almost equal to the 31,000-people working within the European commission. Many thousands of these lobbyists previously worked within the European parliament and by some estimates, 75% of legislation is influenced by these lobbyists. Leaving Europe will not get rid of these lobbyists and their financial influence, merely redirect it in the coming years. There will likely be a substantial increase in political donations in the UK as firms seek to influence policy back home.

Crushing crony capitalism requires taking on these interest groups after Brexit. Brexit is only the beginning of this revolution.

Demolishing the Revolving Door

Lobbyists will never go away. When you ban funding, it goes underground. When you prosecute lobbyists, they change job titles. When you keep them at arms-length they sue you in the courts. However, you can limit their reach and influence over policy, and as always transparency is vital in this battle. The primary step, however, must be "to shut the revolving door" between lobbyist organisations and legislators.

The first move to make would be for all lobbyists to register and to be prohibited from standing for political election for 5 years after working as a lobbyist. Equally and most importantly, elected politicians and top ranking civil servants should be banned from joining lobbyist organisations for 10 years after leaving politics. It is impossible to completely eliminate the power of lobbyists, but we can certainly severely limit their influence.

Licensing Liberalisation

Licenses were designed for an era where consumers had no ability to assess quality, where rogues could cheat people out of their hard-earned dollar or fail to deliver the service they promised. Licenses are still needed in some areas to shut out rogues from sectors where people are particularly unknowledgeable. Clearly it would be very questionable to allow anybody to work as a doctor without qualification, with consumers unaware of the complete lack of education of a surgeon. But why today do you need a license to rent out your house because it has 3 floors and you want to rent it out to a few friends living together? Why do taxi drivers in London need to spend 3 years memorising every street and pass "the Knowledge", when Satellite Navigation renders this irrelevant? Why can't a qualified architect from the USA work as a qualified architect in the UK? Do American building really fall down that much more?

Licensing is the ultimate protection for insiders, crafted and manipulated by lobbying to serve the simple purpose of eliminating competition. Allowing them to exploit consumers and line their own pockets. Licensing is utilised not to protect consumers from rogue professionals, but instead licensing is used by rogue professionals to exploit consumers. In fact, in the UK licensed professionals on average earn 13% more than unlicensed professionals of the same skill level. For instance, and this may shock you, Black cab drivers in London working a 45-hour week earned on average just over £100,000 until Uber arrived and broke their licensed Monopoly. That's right, £100,000 a year for doing something which anyone with a driving license is theoretically capable of.

The sad reality is that for centuries industries have exploited regulators to protect their own cartels. Initially introduced into the UK in 1066 with the Norman Invasion of Britain, guilds sprang up across the country. The Norman legal system required that for peasants and ordinary folk to take part in a skilled trade, whether iron smiths or stone masons, they required the monarch's permission or license. This served no purpose except to protect a privileged class of insiders from ordinary folk and to restrict prosperity. These guilds proliferated and now have become such an entrenched way of life across the globe, that licenses are seen as the norm for skilled professions. It is truly incredible how we have been held back by a policy introduced by an invasion 950 years ago.

Finally, licensing has the cursed effect of holding back innovation. It prevents disruptive innovation from entering in to the sector and thereby hampers productivity. This continues to drive up the relative cost of licensed sectors at the expense of everybody outside of the system. Licensing is not just a conduit of cash for crony capitalists, but also a barrier to a truly entrepreneurial Britain.

To break the crony capitalist cartel, we should look to remove and simplify licenses wherever possible. This means relaxing constraints on who can operate a hotel, who can drive a mini cab or when a shop has to shut. Beyond this, the government should look towards mutually recognising professional qualifications from overseas so foreign educated doctors, scientists, lawyers and architects etc. can practice in the UK and vice versa.

The Agricultural Lobby

The first and most powerful lobby to confront in the UK is the agricultural lobby. Grown fat on Common Agricultural Policy subsidies the agricultural lobby has developed this remarkable narrative that without subsidies nothing would be grown in the UK. The National Farmers Union say that in order for UK agriculture to succeed we need a "Domestic Agriculture Policy" where the government will "maintain the existing level of investment in farming" and on top of this government agencies should be banned from buying foreign food.

This is stark raving madness. The great advantage of Brexit is that farmers will no longer be able to farm subsidies and instead have to farm the produce people actually want. It is not right that farmers are allowed to live off the taxes of every other working person in the country. Farmers are not some poor, marginalised group with low incomes that we should feel pity for. In 2015, the average farmer received £28,300 in subsidies! This means that the average farmer was paid more in subsidies than the average person earns in a whole year in the UK.

Is that fair for the ordinary working Brits to work hard, pay their taxes while one part of society lives off their hard work?

Well hang on, maybe this criticism is unfair. Maybe in return for these subsidies we get cheaper food in our supermarkets?

Actually no. If we removed all barriers to agricultural trade and all subsidies the price of food in the UK would actually fall by 15%. The Common Agricultural Policy distorts agricultural production so badly and taxes foreign goods enough to push up the cost of food. This "food tax" pushes up the cost of food for everyone in this country to subsidise the lifestyles of agricultural landlords.

Contracting Collusion

Some of the most egregious examples of crony capitalism exist not in the private sector, but in public sector contracting out to the private sector. The reason people hate PFI schemes and Public Private Partnerships is not because of a dislike of competition, but in the collusive exploitative nature of public private contracting. Why is it that the same firms always get the government contracts and almost always have cost over-runs?

Looking at defence contracting in particular.

The sad reality, is for years private firms have run circles around the UK government. The UK government, insistent on quality guarantees, have made contracts so complex to comply with that only the largest companies are able and, in some cases, allowed to bid for them. This allows a small cartel of large suppliers to inflate prices at the expense of the British taxpayer. This cartel exploits the lack of negotiating expertise in the UK government to construct contracts with excessive cost overrun provisions, so that the taxpayer foots the cost of any incompetence on the part of the contractor.

The left rightly complains about the profit gouging of private sector firms and the supernormal profits they extract from governments across the world, but jump to fallacious conclusions. They say that the solution is to replace this limited competition with a government monopoly on the naïve assumption that as soon as a manager starts working for the public sector their productivity and motivations are transformed. Sadly, we are all human and respond to incentives in the same way whether publicly or privately owned. Instead, the only way to deliver the public services we deserve is to break these cartels open and expose them to the power of both domestic and foreign competition. All contracts, except those of significant national security concern, should be opened up to any firm, domestic or foreign. Whoever can deliver that service at the highest quality for a given price should win that contract, regardless of their geographic headquarters.

Competition has made this world rich and driven innovation worldwide. Let those same forces transform our public services and we could have the best public services in the world.

CHAPTER 5: BUILDING BRIDGES TO A BRIGHTER FUTURE

> *"A rising tide doesn't raise people who don't have a boat. We have to build the boat for them. We have to give them the basic infrastructure to rise with the tide."* – Rahul Gandhi

There is a reason that every politician you know loves to be seen pictured in a hi-vis jacket on a building site for the latest great infrastructure project. The photo opportunities that Crossrail provided for George Osborne in his tenancy of number 11 Downing Street were almost countless. Sadly, the reality is that over the past decade, investment as a share of GDP has been lower than at any point in our recorded history. Why if they were so politically convenient have we not invested enough in infrastructure, surely there would be overinvestment not underinvestment?

Unfortunately, most infrastructure proposals are politically the least sexy thing a party can propose to the electorate. When one side is proposing a marriage tax break for every married couple in the country and free prescriptions on the NHS, what politician would say that instead of these giveaways we need to pour that money into electrifying the railways across Cumbria and the North East, while investing in boosting the capacity of hidden flood drainage systems across the country. It would be political suicide.

Sadly, the reality is that as voters we tend to have a very short outlook when casting our ballots, we don't think 10 years down the line. However, Brexit offers a small window of opportunity to change this. People on the 23rd of June 2016 voted to take a risk in the short term for a brighter future in the long term. People have been drawn to Corbyn in part because for once a politician is telling them what they don't want to hear. When he disagrees with popular opinion he says it. Straight talking honest politics really has a ring to it doesn't it?

As you may have guessed, I profoundly disagree with Jeremy Corbyn's solutions for the country, but I recognise his political attraction and qualities. This same energy can be embraced to drive real progress in this great country. A great infrastructure plan to build a stronger, fairer more prosperous Britain is both possible and affordable. Long term infrastructure is one of the few things which can be justifiably funded by borrowing, as it lowers the spending needs of future generations. However, it is essential this funding is directed to the areas of most need and not to politicians' vanity projects. In order to identify the need of the future, it is important for us to understand the historical context of where we are now.

A History of Boreholes, Bombs and Bridges

The modern infrastructure we use today has been shaped in 3 core stages: the Victorian Revolution, post war re-construction and the new economic way. All 3 stages distinct in both their ambitions and their triumphs.

We often look back fondly on the Victorian times, as if it was a time of unbelievable technology growth and prosperity. However, it was much more of a mixed bag and the infrastructure built throughout this time is testament to this. The Victorian era's infrastructure boom was driven by the desire to create the most technologically advanced infrastructure possible. In many cases cost was not an issue and even more fundamentally the infrastructure did not need to serve a wider economic cause provided it achieved technological primacy. It was a race of private benefactors to prove the superiority of their technological prowess. Investment followed market demands, flowing into the wealthy mining and manufacturing towns, while the underdeveloped hinterland was left bereft of infrastructure. Nonetheless, the private sector managed to create a rail network spanning 9,817 miles of the country, construct sewer networks in every major town and leave our capital with an underground system which works to this day.

During the 1st World War the UK state seized control of fundamental infrastructure controlling railways, telecoms and shipyards. Under this new world, the UK turned its focus from big transformative infrastructure projects to beginning to solve every day needs of the ordinary people with a large investment in housing by the state. This accelerated in the 1930s as a housing investment surge was used to alleviate the effects of the great depression on the UK. However, the truly transformative investment surge came after World War II. The horrors of the Blitz and the toll of 6 years of war economics had degraded our roads, bridges, buildings and electrical infrastructure. The economy had been completely militarised and de-militarising the economy would take a gargantuan effort.

In 1945, a Labour government was elected promising to transform the UK economy by taking control of the commanding heights of the economy. It promised to rebuild the UK and form a modern welfare state. Using loans from the US government and a reduction in financial support for colonies overseas, the Labour government set about rebuilding a broken Britain shattered by war. Over the next 2 decades under a combination of Labour and Conservative governments, the British government built over 200,000 homes a year, clearing working class "slums" and investing in brutalist housing with gargantuan tower blocks dominating our new cities. Regulating and banning private development in all but the most limited of cases. Top down city planners tore up old communities, replacing them with cities planned in the vision of the city planner. They even went as far as creating whole new artificial towns, such as Milton Keynes. This government intervention allowed people a place to live, provided people with adequate infrastructure, but was remarkably short sighted. The infrastructure that was built was designed for the needs of the post-war generation, but did not consider the needs of future generations, in no way matching the foresight of the Victorian era. Nonetheless, the government managed to provide for the basic infrastructure needs of people regardless of their income level.

This cosy consensus of low quality, but adequate infrastructure and housing for all was shaken by the election of Margaret Thatcher in 1979. In the early 1970s, the economic model of state directed growth had finally stalled, as the limits of government power were nakedly exposed. In response, Thatcher's government embarked upon a radical transformation. Government investment in housing collapsed, while the national champions of infrastructure were privatised. Many redundant railway lines were closed, and unprofitable villages abandoned with a renewed focus on economic efficiency. This purge of mal-investment rid the UK of dilapidated poor functioning capital and finally started to see an improvement in the quality of housing stock. Houses built by private developers for people, the way they wanted it, not some government bureaucrat or town planner decided it to be. Properties were privatised, and we became a nation of DIY homeowners; as ordinary people began living in their own homes, they invested on improving it. The crowdfunded rebuilding and restructuring of our nation had begun. Soon large investment began to follow and formerly deprived areas, such as the London docklands were rejuvenated with shining steel skyscrapers in Canary Wharf and in the City of London. Meanwhile the purge of state investments and the economic collapse of the mines and factories, led to an accelerated decline of the industrial north. As people suffered unemployment and as factories and mines began to close, the state sponsored housing projects began to decay and were abandoned as people moved south in search of work. After this collapse, many of the mining regions fell into decay leaving empty homes, factories and offices behind.

The Thatcherite consensus, may have delivered us far higher quality housing and infrastructure, yet completely failed to deliver the quantity of housing and infrastructure that people and a modern economy needed. But why on earth did the dynamic free market fail to deliver the housing and infrastructure that we needed?

The truth in the case of housing was that the free market was never truly released. Although the government pulled back its own investment in housing, it failed to relax planning laws and remove building restrictions for private builders. NIMBYs across the country were in fact empowered to block development and restrict new housing projects. The reforms needed in our planning system and housing market are so vast that I have dedicated a whole chapter to it, later in this book, antibureaucratic planning. Therefore, in this chapter, I will focus on what has gone wrong with infrastructure investment, or rather lack of investment, and see what might be done to truly transform this great nation.

Infrastructure & the Need for Ambition

For too long in this country we have been playing catch up when it comes to infrastructure investment. We have accepted that the UK can't afford to invest in infrastructure projects for the future growing needs of our country and instead only spends enough to maintain the existing infrastructure. We are fixing potholes, but failing to build the new roads to unclog our traffic plagued regions. More than this, new infrastructure spending is allocated to high growth areas, such as London and the south east on the basis of economic models which assume regional prosperity as given, not a function or result of the infrastructure and spending decisions of previous generations. This means that the limited infrastructure spending that exists is almost solely allocated to the economically successful regions of the country. This infrastructure allocation accelerates the clustering of wealth and further deepens the regional divides, which are one of the greatest challenges the United Kingdom faces. To put this into perspective, the UK government currently spends £1943 on transport infrastructure per person in London, while the North East and North West of the country only receive £220 and £680 per head respectively. This stinks of economic neglect of vast swathes of the United Kingdom and if we are to have a Brexit which works for everybody, not just London, it is vital that this regional gap is closed.

In fact, boosting regional infrastructure spending to London levels across the country may be self-financing, by generating enough additional economic growth and tax revenue to cover the cost of the new infrastructure projects. For example, if you spend £1bn building a new bridge, which saves 250,000 people 1 hour of commuting every day you create 1.25mn hours a week or 62.5mn hours a year which people can spend working. At a rough value of £10/hour, this one off £1bn spend would create £625mn GDP a year. Assuming 40% of the GDP increase is captured in taxes, then £250mn of additional tax revenue would pay for the bridge in 4 years. In fact, the pay back may be even quicker! The £1bn spent on building that bridge also generates tax revenues from taxes charged to the contractor and his suppliers. Assuming again that 40% of GDP increases are captured in taxes, the year the Bridge is built would generate £400mn of tax revenue, pulling down the cost to £600mn. Therefore, the bridge would pay for itself in less than 2.5 years of operation.

Now the example above is just a hypothetical example, and I do not expect you to just read this and accept that an infrastructure boom would be a free lunch without providing any evidence to support this. Yet, in fact, there is a vast array of academic literature supporting the idea that up to a point infrastructure spending boosts growth so much that it is self-financing in the long run. According to the IMF, on average every £1 invested in infrastructure boosts GDP by £1.4.

So how do we change our way of investing to encourage investment in deprived areas and encourage investment for future needs, not just today's needs. To achieve both of these we need to move away from high discount rate passive cost benefit analysis to low discount rate dynamic cost benefit analysis. Now that all might seem like gobbledygook to most of you, however, all these complex terms really mean, is switching to a model which values the gains of future generations more highly and includes the effect of infrastructure projects on each other and their combined benefits. This is more complex to calculate, but by no means impossible and should be within the means of a modern civil service. If you want to understand these terms more deeply please read, as always, the technical economics section at the end of this book.

But these grand ideas don't amount to much unless we identify the areas of need in British infrastructure. If we just end up spending the extra money on roads to nowhere or high-speed internet somewhere no-one wants to live, is there any point? So where do we really fall behind the rest of the world in terms of infrastructure?

Infrastructure Weakness

	Ranking	Quantity	Quantity of 1st Place
Internet mobile download speeds	42nd	26.1Mbps	57.9Mbps
Internet fixed line download speeds	25th	49.9Mbps	156.7Mbps
Water leakage rates vs European nations	6th (of 15)	22%	3%
High speed rail track laid	7th (of 22)	1,377km	22,000km

With clear holes in our infrastructure plan, it is blatantly clear that our infrastructure does need targeted significant investment to take it into the 21st century. Slow internet speeds are a drag on productivity and it is the responsibility of the UK government to correct this lack of investment by British Telecom, who have exploited their position as a natural monopoly to rip off British consumers. Water leakage rates are wasteful and leave the UK with a weakened ability to respond to crises, drought and floods. Road traffic and underinvestment in rail by Network Rail, the UK state rail monopoly, hold back the expansion of growth outside of London. Closing the infrastructure gap could be one of the key solutions to closing the prosperity gap between different parts of the UK.

It is rare for me to propose that it is governments duty to intervene as usually I detest the regulatory overstep of governments, yet in the case of natural monopolies, a government must intervene to correct for the exploitative habits of the monopolist. First off, there is no reason why both the telecom operator "British Telecom" and the line owner "Openreach" should be the same company. In the same way that National Grid was separated from electricity providers, BT should be forced to sell off Openreach and all its network infrastructure. Then once the firms are separate, Openreach should be required to connect 99% of homes to gigabit optical fibre to the home by 2022, or if they cannot, subcontract to a 3rd provider. This way Openreach will ensure that only the least cost effective 200,000 homes in the country will not gain access to ultra-fast broadband. These remaining homes should be offered a £5,000 subsidy towards the cost of installing the line themselves, enabling 3rd party providers to innovate in delivering the ultra-fast broadband the modern economy needs. To enable Openreach to access the capital needed for such a radical expansion, the government could lend Openreach the capital it needed for such an expansion at government borrowing costs. Yes, ultra-fast broadband will be more expensive than the cheaper fibre to the cabinet option proposed by many, but the UK needs to stop playing catch up in terms of infrastructure and start accepting the need to invest in the future.

Infrastructure failure in water is again evidence of a problem of monopolies. Localised private water monopolies have kept prices of water down, but have done so at the cost of an epic underinvestment in pipes and reservoirs. In the eternal hunt for profit, water giants, such as Thames water, have realised that if they cut investment in pipes and reservoirs they will be able to create sporadic water shortages forcing the government to either pay for new investments or allowing the water suppliers to raise the price of water to finance the required investment. This is madness. Ofwat, the UK water regulator, needs to compel all water monopolies to cut water leakage rates by half within 2 years and boost reservoir capacity by 10%. Again, the government can help alleviate the cash crunch of this by lending the money needed for the infrastructure investments. This will be a cost-free investment for the government, which will ensure that we do not face any water crises in the near or medium future.

Finally, the most interesting of the infrastructure improvements that we can embark on is revitalising our road and rail infrastructure. Self-driving cars will be one of the most transformative technologies to emerge in the western world for decades. They will completely change the needs we have from our road infrastructure, as street parking disappears, and cars drive and recharge themselves. With this in mind, it is pointless to plan our changes in road infrastructure without the needs of self-driving cars in mind. In order to address the needs of future road users we must ask what infrastructure do self-driving electric cars need?

1. An extensive network of charging stations where they can automatically charge themselves without human interaction. A potential compromise could be having humans working to plug and unplug rows of self-driving cars once they were full. A key aspect of these charging stations is that they should be interchangeable between electric car models, not reserved for Tesla cars only. The government should contract out to the lowest bidder, the job to install these chargers, which will initially be rented out to the petrol station operators, before being sold off once they are commercially viable. Now this is not just a futuristic pipe dream, this is already being done in the Netherlands!
2. 2+ lane roads with dedicated lanes for cyclists and pedestrians to avoid interactions with the self-driving car network. This would be significantly

more expensive to transform all the small country lanes, so that they are prepared for the self-driving car age, however this could be combined with the rollout of ultra-fast broadband by Openreach and the water infrastructure repairs to minimise disruption for ordinary Brits. Although this will be disruptive
3. Finally, electric cars need a wide telecom network and the government should investigate the most cost-effective way of ensuring that all UK roads have mobile network coverage. On this issue I cannot offer a simple fix.

In contrast, rail infrastructure problems are far clearer to resolve, as we have witnessed successful rail reforms overseas. Rail franchises are deeply flawed because the responsibility for maintaining and operating the track is separated from the responsibility for operating the trains. The current organisational structure has enabled both Network Rail and rail operators to dodge their responsibility to their customers and blame the other. Responsibility for delays is not clear and has damaged trust in our rail services. To restore trust and allow operators to focus on delivering the best service, operators should bid for the responsibility to operate both the track and the trains on top of it. Network rails focus should then switch into shaping the infrastructure that we need for the future and upgrading and building new track. HS2 should go ahead instantly, while fast rail links should be built between all major airports and the local city centres. The government should allocate a £8bn/year investment surge into electrifying existing lines and building new lines, such as the Cambridge-Oxford corridor and the Manchester-Liverpool interchange. This separation of the day to day operations from infrastructure planning is core to this reform.

Finally, I will not address the localised infrastructure changes required in this chapter as these are far better answered in the final chapter on antibureaucratic planning. This will include some proposals for transforming mass transit within our cities and towns. Nonetheless, I hope the proposals above have begun to tickle your mind with ideas of what we can do to upgrade Britain.

CHAPTER 6: A SIMPLE SELECTION OF CHARTS

"It is a capital mistake to theorise before one has data." – *Arthur Conan Doyle*

This chapter contains a series of charts detailing our relationship with the EU and our place in it. I will leave it up to you to come to your own conclusions from the data which I present. The charts contained here are all food for thought, and although you may have seen some of these before in the vast array of Brexit literature, I hope that much of this is new and of interest to you. I have selected 4 charts to highlight the UK's role in the world and our relationship with Europe. The first 2 neatly display our trading relationship with Europe and show how it has evolved over time. The next graph displays how the UK is one of the few nations in Europe who live up to the international obligation to spend 0.7% of GDP a year on Foreign Aid and Development Assistance. The fourth chart highlights the role that the UK plays in the defence of Europe from aggression in the east, as well as fulfilling peacekeeping roles globally. The first charts can be seen overleaf.

Our export dependency on the EU-27 has gradually fallen throughout this period and today only 43% of our exports are destined for EU markets. In contrast, 54% of our imports come from EU nations. In a perverse way, over the past decade we have grown less dependent on the EU for our export earnings while the other EU nations have become more dependent on us for growth. Nonetheless as of today, the EU is still our most important economic partner.

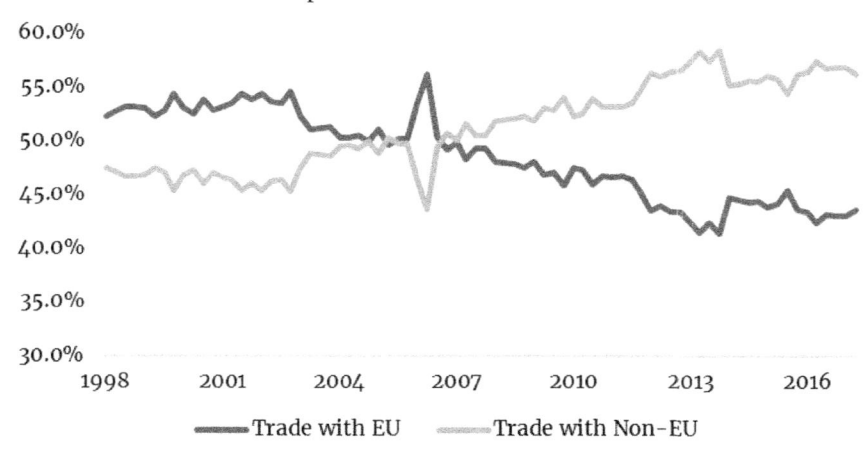

Export Share EU & Non-EU

Import Dependency EU & Non-EU

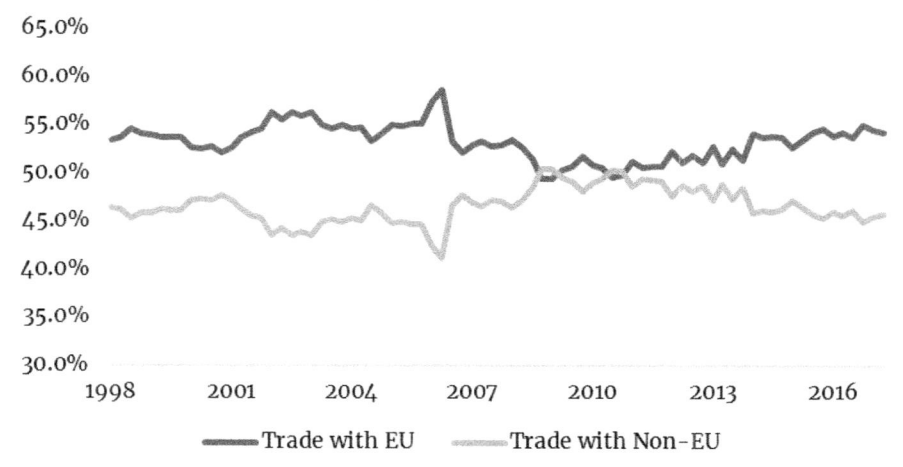

Foreign Aid Spending % of GDP

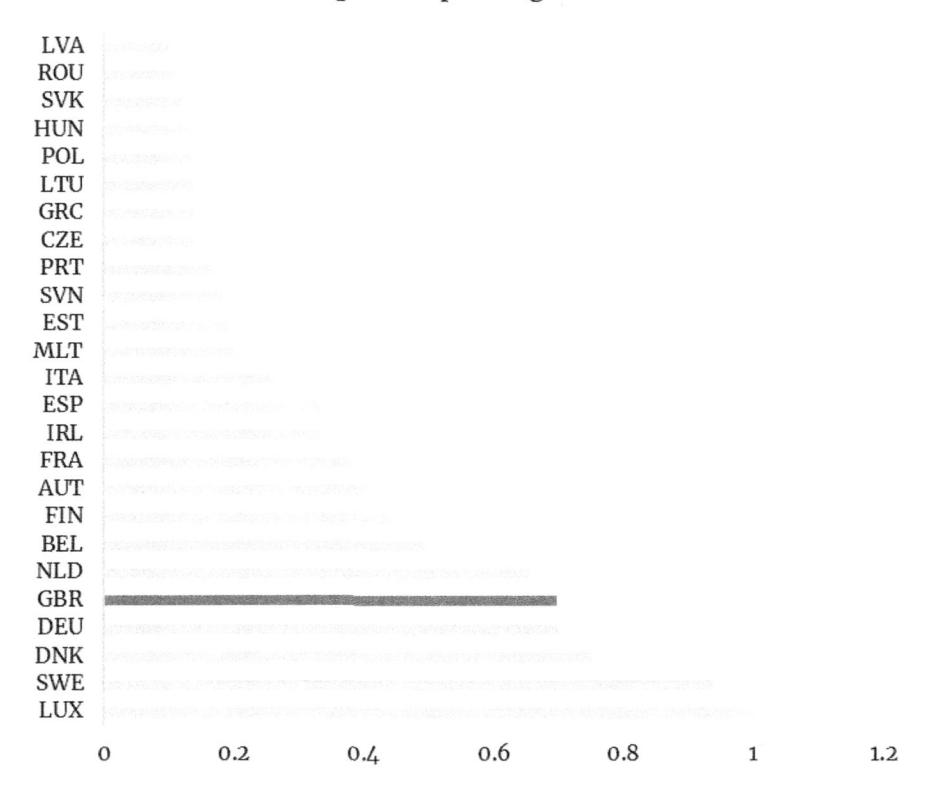

As indicated by the chart above, the UK is one of only 5 nations in the EU who meet their UN foreign aid obligations. The UK spends £13bn a year on foreign aid and is one of the most influential aid powers in the world. Giving back and trying to do right by the world.

Defence Spending

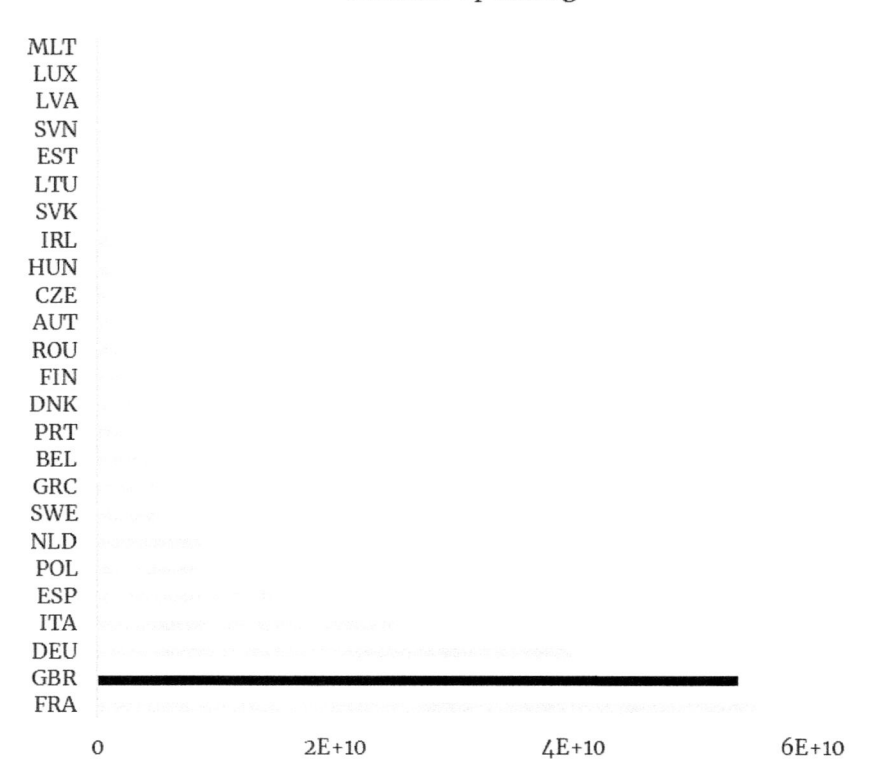

MLT	
LUX	
LVA	
SVN	
EST	
LTU	
SVK	
IRL	
HUN	
CZE	
AUT	
ROU	
FIN	
DNK	
PRT	
BEL	
GRC	
SWE	
NLD	
POL	
ESP	
ITA	
DEU	
GBR	
FRA	

0   2E+10   4E+10   6E+10

The UK and France are the only credible military forces in Europe. Collectively with the US, we have provided the whole of Europe a shield from Russian military aggression for decades.

CHAPTER 7: IMMIGRATION, INTEGRATION AND INNOVATION

They're a racist bunch of troglodytes.

They hate foreigners.

They don't know what they're voting for, they are just voting against immigration.

After the referendum on the 23rd of June, Brexit voting Brits were labelled and castigated as uneducated and misguided. We were blanket stereotyped with many of the above criticisms and were clearly too stupid in the eyes of the "highly educated" elite to make a decision. I have friends on both sides of the debate. Do I think that my Remain voting friends were stupid? Unpatriotic? Un-caring? No, of course not. I think they are wrong in their choice, just as they think I am wrong to support leave.

However, these fears of xenophobia and anti-immigrant ethno-nationalism should not be dismissed out of hand. There was a small, but significant, contingent of Brexit supporters who wanted a whiter Britain. It would be a travesty if these ethno-nationalists hijacked Brexit, to be some perverse Neo-Nazi dream. Our grandparents did not fight to let our country be conquered by this ugly ideology, in fact our country was built on waves of migrants moving for better economic opportunity or fleeing persecution. Whether the Huguenots in the 1680s fleeing religious persecution or the Lascars (Indian scholars) migrating to the UK in the 17th and 18th century, every migrant group has shaped this country to make it what it is today. Including my own ancestors, the Huguenots, fleeing persecution in France. Yet for decades, the immigration system of this countries has been warped and distorted, shutting the door on skilled migrants while having no control on selection for 500mn potential migrants. This has to change. On June 23rd we voted to take back control of our borders from EU bureaucrats and to make decisions here in Westminster about how we select the people who get to reside in our great nation.

Yet, we did not vote to take back powers from EU bureaucrats just to let Whitehall bureaucrats enforce the same rules in the same bureaucratic manner. If we truly want to satisfy the will of the people we must build a migration system which is transparent, non-bureaucratic and works for the interests of the British people. Currently to hire a high skilled expert in artificial intelligence on say £100,000, companies need to prove to the government that this type of skilled worker doesn't exist in the UK or the EU. How on earth does a bureaucrat in the home office know whether that skill exists in the UK or not? They don't! Instead of strangling these companies in red tape, why don't we make an immigration system that works with companies and market signals.

Imagine for a moment that we replaced the current system of bureaucratic visas with a market based immigration system. The biggest challenge with immigration is the burden which some migrants put on public services and the wages of the low skilled. What if we designed a system which ensured that every immigrant paid their way, not just the most skilled? What if we designed a system where migrant labour was no longer able to suppress the wages of low skilled workers who are struggling to make ends meet? What if we could do all this while ensuring that every company who needed a worker would be able to hire that worker with having to a bureaucrat in Whitehall that they needed that worker?

You may think that this is all just a pipe dream, but actually it is totally feasible and realistic. What if, instead of demanding that firms prove through paperwork and legal battles they needed a worker, they bought the right to employ a foreign worker from the UK government? The UK government could charge these companies say £5,000 a year for every worker they sponsored from outside of the UK. This would raise tax revenue for UK public services and ensure that every migrant was a net contributor to the UK. Instead of some migrants being a burden on our public services, every migrant could finance world class public services. Complaints about migration would disappear if people realised that their Pakistani neighbour was paying for the fantastic schools which they were enjoying. Unskilled migrants would no longer be desired by British firms, as unskilled foreign labour would become too expensive to hire. Wages at the bottom would begin to grow, while firms who need genuine skilled labour would have no problem paying £5,000 to get the worker they need. This charge could be varied to limit levels of migration into the United Kingdom, and if population growth really started accelerating, we could increase the charge to tame migrant numbers. However, I would expect in reality, as the gains of skilled migration begins to become really apparent, the British population would actually like to see increasing migration.

We also want a system which enables migrants to engage in entrepreneurialism and build the start-ups which transform this world. At the moment, I see non-European friends who are trapped in jobs unable to try out their start-up idea in the UK and so have to leave the country to start up their companies. Currently visas are so inflexible, that even future entrepreneurs with the savings to launch their idea are unable to take that risk, because they instantly will lose their right to remain in the UK. The exodus of entrepreneurial talent is detrimental to everything we hope to achieve in the UK. These are the people who will build the technologically ground-breaking firms which become the employment engines of the future. So why on earth are we forcing them to leave our country! It is absolute madness and this problem will only get worse after we leave the EU, as more migrants are caught in the bureaucratic machinery of the Home Office. We must design a system with the flexibility for entrepreneurs from anywhere in the world. This system need not be complex and could build on the same principles as the workers migration system proposed above. Prospective entrepreneurs could pay an annual visa fee of £10,000 to be free to live, work and do anything but claim benefits in our fine country. This would weed out entrepreneurs with no financial means and ensure that they will pay for the cost of public services and never be a drain on taxpayer resources.

There is also human concern and the issue of spousal visas and family reconciliation. This is a more complex issue than the system of skill based migration. We want to ensure that British citizens are able to live with their children and spouses in the United Kingdom. However, we must recognise that marital visas in particular have represented a soft back door for migration for years. I personally have several friends & past colleagues who rushed into marriage with their partners in order to ensure that the partner can live and work in the United Kingdom, consciously aware that they may divorce soon after. I wouldn't go so far as calling these sham marriages, but I would say that our immigration system has generated some rather perverse behaviour with "till permanent residency do us part" seeming a more accurate description of many people's marital intentions than "till death do us part". Nonetheless, I believe that the current system is close to the best of a bad bunch of options. Naturally offspring will be able to live in the country due to their birth right to British citizenship, however spousal rights should be restricted to an extent. At the moment a partner only has to prove 1 of the above: they are in a civil partnership/marriage, they are engaged and will marry within 6 months or they have lived together in a relationship for 2 years. I would suggest that the first two options drive up sham marriages and visa abuse, while the 3rd option is a fairly evidential proof that you are in a committed relationship (although again there are flaws). Therefore, I would propose to tighten the spousal visa system by removing the first 2 options.

When dealing with the rights of the partners of British citizens we must not forget the rights of the partners of legal migrants in our country. However, these rights must be balanced against the financial burden of providing public services to the dependents living here. We can again extend the system of annualised visa fees to enable the settling of the families of skilled migrants into this country. Dependents could pay £5,000 for dependency visas, which would grant them the same rights to work and access to public services as entrepreneurship visas. This would not be cheap and mid skilled workers would not be able to bring in large families to join them. However, it is the fairest compromise when balancing the needs of natives, British companies and the interests of migrant communities.

These solutions are elegantly simple, but no solution is perfect and there will still be challenges and strains. No more so than the subject of integration. It is pointless to discuss immigration without talking about the issues and challenges of integrating migrant communities into the cultural framework of the UK. If the question had only been economic, the solution would be simple, however cultural challenges will be far more challenging to overcome. Integrating our migrant communities will require a change in attitudes both on the part of natives and migrants.

Cultural Integration: A Battle for Hearts and Minds

One of the most fascinating realities about modern day Britain is how well migrant communities from 50 years ago have integrated into British culture. Whether the British Indians, Irish, Afro-Caribbean or Chinese minority groups, all have become part of our society. In some ways there is nothing more British than a Chicken Tikka Masala, a concoction designed by Glaswegian Indian curry chefs 50 years ago. As a fun side note, almost all of our "Indian" curry restaurants are actually run by the British Bangladeshi community. However, even these well integrated communities were initially outside of general British society when they arrived. As migration has increased, we have become faster at integrating foreigners into our society, yet not fast enough to prevent the cultural strife that such migration triggers.

So how do we accelerate cultural integration?

Well, the first step to any form of integration process is to break down the barriers between different communities. These non-economic barriers largely come in 3 different types: language, social and structural. As such I will address each barrier in turn. Linguistic barriers create the most obvious barrier. How on earth can people integrate when they don't understand the local language and can't communicate with those outside of their community?

Thankfully linguistic barriers are one of the simplest issues to confront. I have learnt, living in Barcelona, where initially I spoke neither Catalan nor Spanish, that without the local tongue the local community would not open up to me, even though many speak English. However, after learning a little Spanish, suddenly the warmth and acceptance I received from people was unmatched. Every time I spoke my broken Spanish, people would complement me on what I had learnt and put an extra effort in to correct my errors. In just a couple of months, despite working in English, I have gained the ability to fully converse in Spanish with no need to use English. Every migrant in the UK has the exact same opportunity, if they just received that little head start in the beginning. Migrants do not need perfect English, but merely a decent enough grasp that they can communicate. From there, they can learn themselves. Sadly though, some of the more isolated communities don't gain that proper initial grasp of English and therefore never become integrated into British society. We should offer to all resident and new migrants the opportunity to take a month of intensive English courses, or 3 months of part time English courses. Fully funded by revenue from the migration visa fees. By giving migrants the initial immersion in the language, we will open the door to self-improvement to all migrants and bring them into British society creating the social and cultural mobility that this country needs.

The challenge of social integration is far more complex, than the linguistic barriers highlighted above. Social integration requires the erosion of cultural differences to a level where those cultural differences no longer conflict with cultural British values. This requires the rejection of multiculturalism and the assumption that we should just respect and accept people's cultural values however much they differ from ourselves. We must reject multiculturalism, because by respecting cultural views of intolerance, social and sexual hierarchy we remove the idea that there is any morality or value in our own British values. There is something fundamentally right with the idea that men and women are equal; that freedom of speech and expression is sacrosanct and that minorities should be protected from discrimination. This means rejecting fundamentalist Wahabist views that women are 2nd class citizens. That papers should not be silenced for offending Christo-Judean values. That businesses can't refuse to provide a man a service, because they are offended by their sexuality. But how do we spread these British values and overcome the importation of incompatible and backward value systems?

The wrong answer is to follow the lead of some European nations who have chosen to ban the Burka, stop mosque building and closed their door to refugees in their time of need. These persecutions would only serve to drive the more poisonous parts of these ideologies underground. After all, Islamic scholars gave us the hourglass, the decimal system and the foundations of modern medicine. Equally we must not be scared to confront the contradictions with our own dominant Church of England, particularly on gender equality. Open debate and discussion is vital, people need to choose the British value system, school sex education classes should never be optional and religious education must never by focussed on just one religion. Let children go back to their Wahabist parents and ask, "why is mummy never allowed to leave the house unaccompanied?", open up the debate and teach people that these are the values we follow in the UK. If people do not accept the core role of British values and accept the principles of freedom of expression, tolerance and gender equality, then they need to find a society that meets their cultural demands. The UK will not and must never sanction these values as compatible with British principles. I wish I could offer some silver bullet to transform and supercharge the rate of social convergence, but sadly I can't. However, for those who are fascinated by this topic, I have included some academic papers at the end of this book which dig more deeply into this topic.

Finally, we touch on the issue of structural segregation. Structural segregation is where communities do not mix and live together, but instead form ghettoised units, surrounded by members of "their community" while separated from those of different backgrounds. Naturally, structural segregation can never be truly eliminated, as people have always tended to live near those of similar incomes and interests, people who like hockey will naturally coalesce around an AstroTurf, families who like spacious gardens will move out to the suburbs. This isn't social cleansing, but the natural desires of ordinary people. Nonetheless, the structuring of our cities into wealthy and poor areas is clearly detrimental to the social mixing that we hope to achieve. Structural segregation comes in two forms: inertia and active separation. Inertia is driven by the initial setting that people are born into. If a British-Pakistani child is born into a household in the Pakistani areas of Bradford, they are likely to stay near home to be close to family as they grow up. This pull is even stronger among communities where family ties are more important, as they tend to be within migrant communities. With family, the possibility of an inherited family home and a whole support network, inertia is completely understandable. However, inertia is also driven by a second, less attractive set of forces. Economic stagnation of certain regions of the UK trap people into cycles of introversion. When times are really challenging, people migrate to escape. When the economy is booming, people migrate to seize these opportunities. However, when economies are stagnant, people stay in their comfort zones and only the most talented leave. The contrast between the inter-communitarian relations in London compared to my old home area on the outskirts Bradford is remarkable. Economic opportunity breaks down the structural barriers to segregation, as upwardly mobile Bengalis move to the suburbs, breaking up the whitewash of our suburban regions.

Economic opportunity for migrant groups is the silver bullet to overwhelm inertia driven structural segregation. Economic opportunity is driven by 3 core factors: education, economic growth and stickiness of job markets. Fortunately, there are encouraging signs that we have made some of that progress already in the first of these factors. Every single ethnic minority group in the UK outperforms white British nationals throughout secondary school, once you strip out economic differences. However, economic differences have a monumental effect on the performance of all children and minority children tend to come from poorer backgrounds. Correcting this educational inequality gap will require a multitude of policies, which I have laid out already in chapter 2: Building the Great Meritocracy. Economic growth remains far too weak outside London and the South East, and regional gaps must be closed if we hope to have a chance of overcoming the social inertia. Finally, sticky job markets, outside of the public sector, are not a significant challenge for the UK with its liberalised labour markets.

Sadly, though inertia is not the only driver of structural segregation, there is a real and determined undercurrent in some communities to actively segregate themselves. Pressure is put on the young of these families to not just conform with community expectations, but also, never to leave these communities. Social attitude surveys indicate that 42% of Muslims would not want a close family member to marry outside of the community. It would be wrong if our own liberal tendencies enabled communities to create a form of voluntary apartheid. Fortunately, among many young Muslims these viewpoints are changing. Yet sadly, this aversion to mixed race marriage is prevalent today among both whites and some minority groups. More specifically outside of religion marriage is seen as a betrayal of community values within certain groups. This is frankly vile and unacceptable. In some cases, I can only sadly conclude that there are some people in this country who have no wish to integrate or assimilate into British society. I love migration and the great wonders which migrants (including my mother) have brought to this country, yet if they never plan to integrate into British society, they should leave. They aren't welcome here with their backwards social views.

CHAPTER 8: GREEN, LEAN & MEAN MANUFACTURING

The European Union has been widely credited for its environmental forward thinking and its commitment to the environment and combating global warming. Under a tough European regulatory advance, manufacturing across Europe has become greener, as highly polluting industries and competitors were shut down by strict emission standards and other green legislation. They have succeeded in bringing down emissions across the UK to below 76% of Kyoto levels, while economic growth has continued to expand. Cars have grown more efficient and energy wasting appliances & lightbulbs have been scrapped. Overall the EU's track record on reducing emissions production across the Eurozone has been largely successful. Nonetheless, evidence based research demonstrates that the EU's environmental policy has not just disrupted economic growth, but more importantly has done nothing to reduce global greenhouse gas emissions and may have led to the world emitting more carbon dioxide.

Now how on earth could I make such a wild claim? How could environmental emissions standards for EU industry actually harm the environment and the world we live in? Well those polluting factories that we shut down have just moved overseas to countries with little to no environmental regulation and exported even more environmentally damaging goods back to the EU. The UK alone imports goods with a carbon footprint of 391 million tonnes of carbon dioxide, 47% of our whole carbon footprint. The big lie in all the propaganda pushed by the EU is that what matters is pushing down the level of emissions produced in the EU. Whereas in reality what matters is the amount of emissions generated by the stuff we can consume and use. It doesn't matter, for the environment from a planetary perspective, if the steel we use is produced in a factory in Port Talbot or Shenzhen China, it only matters how many emissions are generated in the steel we use. If you look at our carbon consumption, i.e. carbon emissions generated making the stuff we consume in the UK, we find that carbon emissions are unchanged since Kyoto. A complete and utter betrayal of the spirit of the Kyoto protocol.

Now if EU environmental policy has been damaging both for the war against carbon and the manufacturing sector what should we replace it with? I cannot hope to answer this in the proper detail it deserves in a single chapter, never mind in one chapter which outlines the resurgence of UK manufacturing. Nonetheless we can address the 'first principles around which our new regulatory regime should be built. Fundamentally, this regulatory regime should be split into addressing 2 fundamentally different types of pollution & environmental damage: localised environmental damage & supranational pollution.

I won't criticise the EU when has done a good job and in the case of regulating localised environmental damage it has done a pretty damn good job. Combined with the work of the Canal & River Trust, among other bodies, the EU has cleaned up our waterways and rid our rivers of heavy metal pollutants as well as sewage. Deforestation has been abated with forests across the UK growing by 22% over the last 15 years with the introduction of forest support payments. Thanks to EU & UK government efforts we are living in a country with cleaner waterways and a greener landscape. We should base our new local regulatory regime on the existing EU directives, alongside the forest cities plans outlined in the chapter on antibureaucratic planning.

Supranational pollution control in contrast has been utterly ineptly managed by EU authorities because of a simple lack of understanding of the economics of production. Adopting over-simplistic models, many environmental regulatory calculations have assumed that the EU is a closed economic system with no trade or capital flows with the outside world. Under this assumption, we could ignore the effect of regulation on the competitiveness of European manufacturing. However, the real world is not the same. Increasing environmental regulation on production plants can raise the costs so that a plant is no longer profitable if based in the EU, and so either the company fails or it moves manufacturing overseas to nations with little or no environmental regulations. This has the perverse effect that by making already strict emission standards harsher and more onerous, the net result is an increase in emissions, as manufacturing plants move overseas. If instead of punishing production of greenhouse gasses, we found a way to punish the consumption of the same products, we would find a way of reducing production of both domestic and imported polluting goods.

The solution is actually remarkably simple in concept, but far trickier to actually implement. We should impose a carbon added tax on all products & services bought & sold in the UK. Modelled on the VAT, this tax would levy a £40 tax for every tonne of carbon dioxide emitted in the production of a good or service. At every stage of the supply chain the tax would be charged on every additional tonne of CO_2 emitted. If the good would be exported the tax would be refunded, as that good would be being consumed overseas. In contrast every good or service imported would face a tax on the amount of CO_2 produced in the making of that product. In one fell swoop no company would have an incentive to offshore manufacturing & jobs in order to sell into the UK. Companies could no longer avoid paying for the damage they were doing to the environment, by moving jobs overseas. In addition, this one measure would raise £44bn of tax revenue for the UK government from the 1100 million tonnes of CO_2 consumed.

Now practically, the imposition of this tax would face one big issue, import emission measurement. Initially, the practical implementation of a carbon emissions tax would rely on other countries having an accurate and reliable system of measuring carbon emissions at production. This would be a pipe dream for the less developed countries. A short-term fix could be to tax imports on the basis of average emissions to produce such a product, as it is much more feasible to measure the average level of emissions of a product produced outside of the UK. This could be done by assuming that foreign imports have the same level of energy use and inputs as the global average, the energy use could then be multiplied by the carbon density of electricity use to calculate average carbon emissions. Please see equation below.

$$CAT = t_{CAT} \times x \times E[e_x] \times d_{e,c}$$

Key

$t_{CAT} = tax\ rate\ per\ tonne\ of\ CO_2$
$x = tonnes\ of\ product\ produced$
$E[e_x] = estimated\ electricity\ use\ per\ tonne\ of\ x\ produced\ (MWh)$
$d_{e,c} = emission\ of\ CO_2\ per\ MWh\ of\ energy\ use\ in\ country\ of\ export$

For instance, let us take the example of mining a tonne of iron ore produced in Mongolia and Norway. Mining that tonne of iron ore in Norway would use 10MWh of energy, which would produce no emissions in Norway, thanks to the hydroelectric power supply used, so no tax would be levied. In contrast, a tonne of iron ore from Mongolia, would be produced using an estimated 10MWh of energy from 100% coal fired power stations, producing 2 tonnes of CO_2 and a tax bill of £80 for importing it.

Now this calculation method will be less accurate for more niche products, such as toy soldiers or Lego bricks. However, it is better to have a slightly inaccurate tax on Carbon emissions than having none whatsoever.

This Carbon Added Tax or CAT, can be replicated and adjusted for all other major pollutants. These emissions taxation schemes would not only raise significant amounts of revenue for the UK government, paying for tax cuts and investments in our public services. It would also allow the UK to play a leading role in the protection of our planet, without punishing British manufacturing.

Now such schemes may face objections from other countries on the grounds that it is merely a form of protectionism. No doubt polluting nations such as China will howl and complain to the WTO, that this is a violation of the terms of tariff non-discrimination. We will need to respond to these allegations carefully, in order not to provoke nations we wish to sign deep trade deals with and so that we may build deep meaningful foreign relations. We should propose to other nations that they should join us and introduce their own CAT in the battle against climate change.

Combating climate change and environmental degradation will never be possible without the birth of a new manufacturing model. For all the wonders of the current model, the sad truth is that it is completely and utterly unsustainable. As we led the world into the first Industrial Revolution, we should see it as our duty to release the new industrial age onto this world. The new Carbon Added Tax could become one of the pillars upon which Britain's New Industrial Revolution will be built, yet there are two more core steps that we need to attain.

As a first step we should ensure that all hi-technology and green technology is allowed into our shores without tariff. We need the UK to have access to all the core component parts needed for a hi-tech manufacturing sector. These new factories should expand well beyond the free tariff ports proposed in chapter 3 and into the wider United Kingdom. By unleashing foreign competition in the hi-tech space onto UK companies we force them to innovate, adopt or die.

The second stage would be to ensure that there is sufficient demand from early adopters for these hi-tech products. The long supply chains will never develop unless there is enough investment demand for these UK sourced hi-tech products. These strong demand chains are vital to develop these self-sustaining industrial clusters, such as the consumer electronics cluster in Shenzhen China. Stimulating these demands should be a priority for UK government, one way in which to achieve this would be to allow companies to expense any investment for tax purposes instead of depreciating it over several years. Private firms would be incentivised to use up their cash piles and invest in the latest machinery and productive assets overnight.

Combined with the 3rd pillar of the Carbon Added Tax, investment expensing and hi-tech tariff elimination could trigger an industrial renaissance across the United Kingdom in clean, green & lean manufacturing. UK manufacturing doesn't need more taxpayers' money or subsidised loans to finance an industrial renaissance, just sensible economic policy, which doesn't purposelessly sacrifice British competitiveness on the altar of environmentalism.

CHAPTER 9: FINANCIAL REVOLUTION

The economic system we have grown to know over the past 3-4 decades was rocked to its core by the Great Financial Crisis of 2007. A system which had generated so much wealth in the past and had apparently delivered us the end of "boom" and "bust", was teetering on the brink of collapse. The level of leverage and exposure of ordinary people to the financial system had grown to a scale 2x larger than the Wall Street Crash of 1929. To say that we were fortunate to have avoided a more brutal global depression than the 1930s would be an understatement. Looking back, it is in fact remarkable how quickly and effectively public policy makers acted to save both the global financial system and the wider economy. Yet, just because we saved ourselves from financial catastrophe before does not mean that we should ignore this opportunity to reshape the financial system for the 21st century.

Finance since the 2nd world war has been shaped by extensive government intervention across the globe. Unlike its reputation, finance is not a freewheeling free market driven sector. It is a rather perverse oligopolistic, state directed form of crony capitalism. Some of the worst excesses have not been driven by rational free agents responding to market incentives, but by a government insurance program where large losses would be nationalised, while all gains would be kept privately by the bankers and their shareholders. This government insurance had been designed to reduce the risk of bank runs and small bank collapses, but had actually created more systematic risk than anyone ever anticipated.

So why on earth does this matter for the UK and what can we possibly do to change this system for the better by ourselves?

London is, to this day, the greatest International centre of finance in the world and the breakthroughs in financial technology that have been made are more advanced than any nation on the globe. London can lead the world in creating a safer banking system, but it needs to be done in a way that does not harm London's competitiveness as a financial hub. The answer to this is intelligent deregulation, which recognises the structural implications that regulation can actually make the financial system far riskier. Not safer.

This may seem counterintuitive to many of you reading this. After the post crisis narrative took hold, the idea that excessive government intervention played any part in weakening the financial system was almost heretical. Nonetheless, I hope to explain how some parts of government intervention weakened the banking system and then will go on to explaining the reforms that could maintain London's position as the leading financial centre of global commerce and become the safe core of the new financial world order.

I recognise that much of this may be quite complex for readers without a financial background, so will go for a back to basics explanation.

Bank Runs

Our modern banking regulatory system was designed with one core goal. Whatever the economic situation, whatever financial pressures emerged, ordinary savers would remain confident that their money was safe at the bank. This was because if savers believed that there was a chance that their bank might fail, then they would respond by withdrawing all their savings. This very action would push the bank into a liquidity crisis where it would run out of freely available cash and be unable to pay out deposits. This would then force the bank to sell their loans on at cut price rates to raise cash, weakening, if not bankrupting the bank. And so this self-fulfilling prophecy ends with a healthy bank driven to collapse by the panic of depositors.

The genius solution to this was for the government to guarantee the savings of ordinary people left in banks. This deposit guarantee program was so elegantly simple. Bank collapses were almost always driven by depositors losing confidence, not because banks became insolvent/bankrupt. This policy would cost governments nothing and guarantee confidence in the banking system.

Nationalising Failure

Except for when the banking system suffered an actual insolvency shock. In 2008 banks such as RBS were about to collapse, deposit insurance could only protect banks from a liquidity crisis, it couldn't protect these banks from insolvency. These banks had simply lent too much money to people and companies who could not pay these loans back. As the defaults on these loans came in, bankers realised that they were bankrupt, they could not afford to pay back their depositors and were going to fail. Suddenly the government and taxpayer was going to have to pay all of the savers in these banks to cover for the mistakes of the banks. How much was this going to cost? Where were governments going to find the money? Had we just nationalised failure?

Deposit protection was a policy designed to both protect ordinary people from the damage of bank failures and to ensure that no bank would ever suffer a bank run. However, by removing all risk from ordinary savers, the government had removed all reason for the banks to keep risk under control. Banks began to pour money into high risk loans, caring solely about maximising their potential return, instead of using these short-term profits to boost their capital reserves. Banks hiked dividends and paid extortionately high bonuses to keep "talent" at the expense of both their shareholders, but more importantly ordinary taxpayers who would pay for the failure. Banks capital levels shrunk, even as their holdings of risky loans ballooned.

The very policy designed to create banking stability had stimulated the largest expansion of casino banking of modern time with cheap debt offered to anyone who wanted it.

So how do we fix it? How do we insure that never again will banks be freely insured to gamble with the taxpayer's money?

Recapitalising Banks

The answer in some ways is elegantly simple. Banks need to be punished for holding insufficient capital, banks should always have enough capital that they can cover the cost of their own failures. Much focus has been placed on this requirement by central banks across the world. However, it is also a reality that capital is expensive for banks to raise and the current system of capital requirements are horrifically inflexible. Now I apologise in advance, but this is about to get highly technical.

Capital comes in two forms: equity and convertible debt. Equity is the simplest form of capital that a bank can raise; equity is simply the bank owning more cash and loans than it owes savers in deposits. If a bank is low on equity, it can sell new shares to raise cash. This cash is then used to lend out as mortgages and other types of loans. As long as the value of the assets (loans & cash) a bank owns is more than its liabilities (debts to other banks & deposits owed to savers), then the bank has equity. The larger the amount of equity, the less risky the bank is. Alternatively, a bank can issue COCOs, which are effectively convertible debt. This means that instead of borrowing from savers or another bank, the bank can borrow through COCOs. These COCOs will automatically be changed from debt to shares in a bank, if the equity levels of a bank fall below a certain percentage of assets. This means that a bank which has too much debt can cancel part of this debt automatically without causing financial contagion. Investors who lent money to banks through COCOs knew that their loans might be turned into shares one day. This means that as long as a bank has enough COCOs issued they will not go bust and the UK taxpayer will never have to pay a penny to bail them out.

Now why on earth am I trying to explain to you what a COCO is? Why don't banks just raise more cash by issuing new shares? The reason is simple. Raising money from shareholders is incredibly expensive for banks and for their customers. We don't want to design a fix to the banking system where customers won't be able to afford their mortgages anymore or businesses can't get the loans they need. This will require compromise and COCOs are part of this compromise, a cheap form of bank financing that will make banks healthier and safer!

Furthermore, we should reward those banks who make their balance sheets stronger than the minimum (4.5%), we should reward banks which do the right thing not just punish those who put the system into risk. For instance, we could scrap the banking corporation tax surcharge, rewarding banks with profitable productive divisions and raise the money instead through a new and improved banking levy. This levy would be charged to all banks with lower than 25% capital levels, the charge would be levied on how much equity they are short of the 25% target. Banks which are well capitalised and safe would pay nothing and pay less corporation tax, while those with risky balance sheets would have to pay the levy as a compensation to the taxpayers who may have to bail out the bank in the future. Think of it like charging the banks an insurance premium, just like your own car insurance. If you're an 18 year old boy racer with little experience and a Ferrari you will pay more than a 40 year old Mum in a reliable Volvo estate. With banks the calculations are a little more complex, but the logic is the same!

These simple steps would make the system considerably safer than in its current state and would allow for the state to stop micro managing aspects of finance. Once the system is safe, we can unleash the innovative potential of the industry to transform the world around us!

The Great Liberation

While banking mis-regulation and government intervention weakened the stability of our financial system over decades, the system we have half replaced it with, has done little to de-risk the system and it has ensured that the financial system has become expensive for people and businesses by protecting incumbents from competition and creating financial oligopolies. Of course, these banks will remain too big to fail if we don't allow smaller firms to come in and steal their market share. Financial regulation has become so expensive to comply with that smaller firms can't even afford to enter the market to compete. Why else have we got to the stage where you can do 24-hour shopping, drinking, eating or working, but branches are only ever open in the middle of the day. Why does it still cost 3-4% to change currency in most banks, when it costs banks 0.05% to trade the currencies themselves?

Fortunately, despite these regulatory hurdles, some challengers such as Revolut and Metro Bank have stepped in to try and shake up the cosy cartel of financial services. But this could change far more rapidly and dramatically than many expect if these regulatory hurdles were torn down. The regulatory liberation could create good high paying jobs across the UK and solidify the UK's stance as the financial capital of the world. More importantly, in some ways, liberating Finance would help to close the financial inequality gap which exists in the UK. Currently normal people, technically known as retail investors, are "protected" from investing in certain types of financial assets. These assets are seen as too risky or "sophisticated" for normal people and can only be sold to the super rich, technically known as professional investors. Even worse, many experts running people's pension funds and investments are banned from investing in these "riskier" assets with retail clients' money. In fact, retail money can usually only ever be invested in highly liquid assets which can be bought and sold within a week.

Now Why is this Unfair and Why Does this Deepen Inequality?

These "protections" or, in reality, restrictions/bans, leave ordinary people locked out from the most profitable investments of all. The rich can invest in illiquid high return private equity and venture capital, while normal folk can only ever pick highly liquid stocks, cash and bonds. Over time this simply means that the rich make higher returns and the rich get richer at an ever-increasing rate. Government is making the rich richer and poor poorer by banning ordinary people from accessing the same opportunities as the rich. This has continued to reduce the returns for pension schemes in the UK as regulations continue to force trustees to invest in low return investments.

Now many people defend this stance by saying many people need to be protected from themselves. People don't actually know what they want and if we leave them alone they'll just be exploited and manipulated. Yes, this may make sense for my 80 year old granny living out in Denmark who gets confused by her computer. But why on earth does this make any sense for a young manager in Sainsbury's who is looking to invest money to save up for a house. Perhaps even more shockingly, this very system of limiting the accessibility for ordinary people actually boosts systematic instability and increases the financial risk of the world we live in.

Yes, that's right. Financial consumer "protection" has increased the instability of the financial system, putting the general economy in jeopardy. This occurs due to the European regulator's obsession with retail investors' "right" to liquidity, rather than their "right" to enjoy good returns on their savings. Investments are by their nature differing in terms of liquidity, so how can regulators say that they must all be liquid? Houses and cars are reasonably liquid, you can usually sell each of these at a fair price within a month of putting them up for sale. Financial assets such as currencies, gold and shares in companies are even more liquid and are possible to buy and sell within minutes if not seconds. In contrast, real world assets can be highly complex; how do you price and sell quickly a beer distilling technology which has a patent for 5 years but no known market yet? You can't. Many productive assets in this world can be highly illiquid and hard to buy and sell, but are vital and useful for the functioning of our economy. What happens when ordinary people are only allowed to invest in liquid assets? Pension funds and asset managers either have to stop investing in any productive illiquid assets or they invest in them but guarantee to their investors that they can pull their money out in a couple of days. So, what happens when funds owning illiquid (hard to sell) assets have to sell these assets to pay out their investors. Either they can't or they trigger a monumental collapse in the price of an asset, devastating other investors in the fund. New papers have in fact suggested that liquid funds holding these sorts of assets can collapse because of a liquidity crisis, much in the same ways that bank runs can happen as detailed above.

The worst offender is the European UCITS directive. Now again I'm going to have to apologise for getting a bit technical and stuck down in the weeds, but this piece of legislation is a key driver in how the European Union has not only made us poorer, but also less stable than before. The UCITS directive funnels retail investors' money into super liquid UCITS funds. The great promise of these structures was that investors in these funds can get their money out from these funds the next day. This ultra-liquidity forces fund managers to conduct fire sales of assets whenever an investor chooses to pull out money. These fire sales push down the price of the assets being sold, lowering the value of the fund as a whole. Investors then can panic and pull out their money. Ultimately this "follow the leader" strategy leads to a self-fulfilling prophecy where the panic forces the fund to collapse and the price of the underlying assets spiral downwards.

Excess liquidity does not just damage investment returns and the risk of "fund runs" (detailed above), it also completely messes up the decision making process within these liquid investment vehicles. Investors pay fund managers management and performance fees so that they can invest their money more effectively than the market as a whole. This requires fund managers to make bets against the markets and take an active opinion on the assets they invest in. When these bets go right, the fund manager makes money for his investors and they pile more money in; when he loses money, they pull money out. Fund managers are rewarded for good performance with more assets to manage, and punished for bad performance. However, what happens if these investment decisions are no longer driven by logical reasoning, but instead by pattern spotting systematic strategies. In particular, what happens if these strategies rely just on the momentum of prices. What if these strategies buy the financial assets which went up in value last month and sold those which went down last month? Crazy, right? Who on earth would design a strategy which has no actual logical reason to buy, just that they buy or sell based on what happened to prices before? In fact, this type of simple systematic strategy is the most common active fund investment strategy. These strategies aggravate market cycles, as investors pile money into the same "successful" strategies and then pull their money out as soon as the strategies start to underperform. This has gradually led to stock markets being driven by technical factors, instead of by fundamentals and the genuine performance of the underlying companies. As long as retail money is piled into liquid investments instead of well thought out illiquid assets, stock markets and the fund management industry will fail in their fundamental purpose in the capitalist system to allocate capital efficiently.

The fundamental misguidedness of major parts of European consumer protection policy has even further consequences for the economic health of the UK. This is because this EU policy distorts the allocation of capital from its most efficient allocation, by driving investment away from illiquid assets into liquid assets. This damages the most fundamental role of financial markets, which is to allocate capital in the most efficient way. Capital misallocation means that factories which should be built don't get built, destroying well paid jobs. It means that new technologies don't get financed and technological advance is slowed. These policies radically slow the advance of our world and limit our economic potential. Leaving the EU can allow us to rid ourselves of this ludicrous drive for excessive liquidity.

If only the lunacy of EU financial regulatory policy stopped at this drive for excessive liquidity, maybe they could be forgiven. Sadly, the EU's populist regulatory agenda has introduced far more ludicrous policies that constrain EU prosperity and weaken the financial services industry. The list of flawed policies is far too long to address in just 1 book, never mind 1 chapter, nonetheless I shall highlight 3 of the most damaging pieces of EU legislation.

1. The Capital Requirements Directive IV (CRD IV) which forces banks to hold excessive amounts of share equity capital, costing our economy £4.6bn a year.
2. The Alternative Investment Fund Managers Directive (AIFMD) which traps hedge fund managers in red tape, while doing nothing to increase access to European markets. These costs act as a tax on savers and investors, costing the UK economy £1.5bn.
3. The Bankers Bonus Cap was meant to punish bankers for their bad behaviour by limiting bonuses at 100% of salary or 200% with shareholder approval. However, instead of pushing down bankers pay, banks responded by massively boosting bankers base pay. Before the reform, during economic slowdowns or hard times, banks could cut bonuses and cut bankers hours from 100 hours a week to 60-70 hours. Now instead, as so much of their pay is in base salary, in crises banks have to fire thousands of bankers. I have personally felt the pain of this, when I was one of 2,000 made redundant in my bank due to weak demand.

A Replacement Model

Replacing this system will not be an overnight job and neither will it be simple to build a replacement. Yet there are a few easy wins which we can achieve at little to no cost to the treasury or regulators. Simply allowing retail investors to invest in illiquid assets, would start to correct the imbalance of excess capital allocation to liquid assets and boost returns for ordinary savers. More specifically illiquid investment funds should be allowed to market to any investors provided they inform savers that their investment will be hard to buy and sell. The FCA should approve a new retail fund type, a RIF (Retail Illiquid Fund). This fund would be allowed to invest in any type of underlying investment only with restrictions on leverage (how much debt can be borrowed by the fund to finance investment). Investors' money should be locked in for a minimum period, say 5 years, after which investors are able to pull their money out. This simple move would allow fund managers to do their job and select the best investment decisions, not follow the market. It would allow ordinary people to invest in the same things that Bill Gates or the Queen can, finally starting to close the gap between rich and poor.

Next, we need to have a bonfire of superfluous EU regulations: removing the 3 regulations highlighted above, would boost the flexibility and vibrancy of the UK financial services sector. It would lower the costs to savers and boost lending and investment across the UK economy. Banks & funds would be strengthened, and when deciding whether to locate within the EU or the UK, financial firms and their high paying jobs would flood into the UK. Leaving the EU, we can offer the British people an opportunity for a revitalised healthy economy.

In order to regain competitiveness & create a banking system which works for all in a post Brexit Britain, regulatory change alone will be insufficient. We need to change the way we extract money from the banking system to reward responsible banking and punish financially destabilising casino banking. Scrapping the additional corporation tax surcharge on bank profits and the bank levy will cost the HMRC £4bn a year or £62 per person in the UK. The banking levy punishes UK banks who lend to ordinary safe borrowers by taxing their balance sheet (i.e. their outstanding loans & mortgages), while the additional corporation tax rate puts our well run banks at a competitive disadvantage internationally. In fact, the bank levy encourages banks to make high risk loans to cover the costs of the levy charged on all assets. Taxing low levels of bank capital in contrast, would make the banking system vastly more stable, while raising the same amount of money. Currently banks hold, on average, capital levels of 6.8% of assets. With £3.9tn of assets, banks are £515bn short of the 20% target level. Therefore, if banks were charged a risk levy of only 0.8% on their capital shortfall, we would be able to raise the £4bn to cover the tax gap from scrapping the banking levy and corporation tax surcharge.

This chapter may have been a little more technical than the others, but I hope it gave you a little insight into the madness of aspects of European financial policy.

CHAPTER 10: TRUE TAX REFORM

"In this world nothing can be said to be certain, except death and taxes." – Benjamin Franklin

Tax harmonisation. Sounds unbelievably dull, doesn't it. The technocratic word for different countries charging their citizens the exact same rates of tax as the other countries, so that no person can be influenced by taxes in deciding where they live and where they locate their businesses. Yet, as with any regulation, tax harmonisation has a darker side. It can kill innovation. Orchestrated tax policy across the EU has failed to keep up with creative lawyers & accountants, who have devised ever more complex and crafty schemes to cheat the taxman out of deserved revenues. In particular multinational corporations have avoided far too many of their obligations to the people of Britain, leaving the rest of us taxpayers to pick up the tab. But in one way, I suppose, we shouldn't blame the player but the game. Why on earth have we let the system of rules be set up in such a way that the wealthiest can use creative debt, leasing & internal pricing strategies to shift profits to low tax jurisdictions, while the rest of us pay our fair share. You don't need to believe in high taxes to see that there is something wrong with this system. I will not criticise the EU for having undermined government efforts to collect tax from corporations and the super-rich, as they have tried to confront tax dodging strategies such as the "double Irish", however, leaving the EU will enable us to become far more creative at confronting tax avoidance.

In this chapter, I will dive into the reforms needed to our corporation tax system to radically reduce tax avoidance, while making the UK the best place in the world to do business. In order to understand what needs to be done, I'm briefly going to explain the 3 core methods under which corporations avoid paying their fair share. These are: transfer pricing, debt & leasing.

Transfer pricing is simply the price at which companies buy & sell services & goods within their own departments. In reality, transfer pricing is only an accounting exercise, it has no real effects, except for the amount of profit a company records in each country it operates in. If companies want to minimise profits in high tax areas and maximise them in low tax areas, all they have to do is make the transfer price of goods flowing from high tax areas to low tax areas really low and then all the profits will be recorded in the low tax area. For instance, let's say Google UK makes £1bn of revenues in the UK and has UK staff costing £100mn; in addition they use patents held by Google Cayman Islands. The Cayman Islands has a 0% corporation tax, while the UK has a 19% corporation tax rate. If the Cayman Islands sets the cost of the patent used in the UK at £900mn, Google can reduce its tax bill by £171mn. There are accounting rules put in place to try and stop this exploitation of transfer pricing for tax purposes, by stating that all internal transfer prices must be priced at the same rate as they would in the open market. But how on earth do you price an internal technology that a tech firm owns and uses internally but never supplies to the outside market? The reality is you can't. Not only is it hard to calculate, but expensive to enforce, even in its deeply flawed state, with HMRC spending £3.8bn a year collecting taxes.

Fiddling with debt is the next most favoured option for companies to avoid tax. Almost every company across the UK employs debt in some way to erode their corporation tax bill. Companies can choose to raise money through 2 core means: debt or equity. Either they raise money from shareholders and pay corporation tax on their profits and dividend tax on their pay-outs to investors or they borrow money from shareholders and backs and deduct the interest off taxable income, shielding themselves from corporation tax. Even more creatively, companies can create internal company loans to lower the profit in one division and move profits to a lower tax country. The current system encourages companies to take on an excessive amount of debt. Stressing the balance sheets of many companies and exposing them to financial collapse in the next recession. Forcing many of the employees into unemployment because of no fault of their own!

The final common trick used by corporates to minimise their tax bill is called sale & leaseback. Companies sell assets owned by a UK entity to a foreign entity located in a low tax country. The foreign low tax country then leases the asset back to the UK entity at a high rental rate. This rental arrangement shifts earnings from the UK entity to the foreign low tax entity. As you've probably realised by now, almost all of the tactics employed by corporates across the UK to reduce their tax bill include shifting their earnings overseas. But what if we could change the system of tax collection so that these outside payments could no longer be deducted? How would companies collapse their tax bills.

A brilliant Oxford based economist, Michael Devereux, came up with an elegantly simple replacement to the current corporation tax system to achieve just this. The Destination-Based Cash Flow Tax (DBCFT), otherwise known as the Border Adjustment Tax. Instead of taxing companies on the basis of where their production resources were, companies would be taxed based on where the revenues were earned. The tax collected on profits earned by German Audi sales in the UK, would be collected in the UK not in Germany. Under such a system any imports into the UK could not be expensed for corporation tax purposes, while exports by UK companies would not count towards revenue. Effectively we would start taxing importers and stop taxing exporters. In addition, interest on debt would no longer be tax deductible for corporation tax purposes. In one fell swoop, transfer pricing manipulation, debt fiddles and dodgy lease arrangements would be pointless and have no effect on corporate tax revenues! That is the magic of leaving our source based taxation to a destination based system.

Actually, the advantages don't just end there. The DBCFT may be the best option for making UK manufacturing competitive again. By switching the burden of corporation tax from UK exporters to imports from foreign firms, we make it cheaper to manufacture and export from the UK. Companies looking where to locate their new manufacturing plants in Europe will trade off between the UK and other European bases and see that the UK offers them 0% taxation on their exports. As the UK is a country with a net trade deficit, such a change would have the added benefit of boosting tax revenues, by collecting more in taxation on foreign imports than would be lost on stopping taxes on UK exporters. In fact, this simple change while holding the tax rate at 19% would raise around £7.2bn of additional revenues, ignoring the increased economic growth from the increased competitiveness of UK exporters. These revenue gains could be even more dramatic if we removed the tax deductibility of interest for corporate profits. Removing debt interest deductions, could overnight eliminate the ability for companies to evade tax by loading UK firms with debt, owned by an offshore subsidiary, such as Google Cayman. Companies have genuine reasons for taking on debt, to finance new investments in plants & machinery and to finance their everyday business, but too often companies take on debt just to lower their tax bill. And tax avoidance is never the right reason for a business decision. Removing this would not only remove the incentive for firms to overleverage and put their workers at risk, but also bring in much needed tax revenue to the government in these times of austerity. In fact, scrapping the corporate interest deduction would raise £15.2bn of additional revenue and lose £5.1bn other tax receipts from the growth deduction.

There is little doubt that such a radical change would struggle to gain adherents in the vested interests of existing national or EU tax authorities, but the noise for change is growing and political pressure may demand action is taken to ensure that corporations pay their fair share of tax!

Corporation tax change is only the first step of making a tax system which works for everyone and restores British competitiveness, but it's a good start. It also represents a quick win and usefully helps raise revenues to pay for the elimination of the most damaging taxes, while leaving a little bit of spare cash to alleviate the pain of other necessary but challenging changes. It would be impossible to finance a modern welfare state without the level of taxation that we have in the UK, however, we can diminish the damage that these taxes inflict on the economy by making some slight adjustments. The most damaging of these taxes are cascade taxes. Cascade taxes are charged on every transaction made, regardless of whether the transaction has made anyone richer. This means that taxpayers are punished for frequent transactions, killing off transactions which would make everyone richer. Stamp duty is a perfect example of cascade tax madness. Let's say that a family of four are looking at buying a 3-bedroom house in Luton and they are able and willing to pay £405,000 for it, meanwhile the retired couple living there would like to move out and are willing to sell for £400,000 (before estate agent fees). In a market with no stamp duty, the family would buy the 3-bedroom house at a price between £400,000 and £405,000 and everybody would be happy. Even better, estate agents would make their commission, removal men would be employed, and small-town lawyers would get a few hours more paid work. Jobs would be created, homeowners happier and retirees richer. Sadly, though the UK government would impose £10,000 of Stamp Duty on such a sale. The family can't afford the £410,000 to buy the house and a beneficial economic trade never happens. No other tax is so damaging. In fact, Stamp Duty Land Tax is estimated by the Adam Smith Institute to be 8 times as damaging to economic activity as VAT and causes £10bn of economic damage, on top of the £12bn that it takes away from taxpayers every year. Scrapping Stamp Duty Land Tax is estimated to generate so much economic activity that other tax receipts would raise £7.5bn extra. This is a low costing tax reform that would generate significant economic activity, £160 of economic activity per person in the country.

Following on from this, I rarely am in the position to say that the financial services sector is being mistreated, but I will make an exception for the case of Stamp Duty Reserve Tax, otherwise known as Stamp Duty for shares. SDRT is another cascade tax which destroys economically valuable transactions, it reduces the returns of pensioners and is a tax on those who stay onshore and pay their fair share of taxes. Before you think that there must be some logic in these taxes and that surely you're missing something, I promise you, you are not. Stamp Duty exists as a result of historical accident rather than a conscious thought of governments. It was introduced when governments had almost no other way of raising revenue, as they had no idea what the incomes were that their subjects made. In fact, Stamp Duty was introduced in England on the 28th June 1694 in order to finance one of our many wars with France. Later on, the introduction of Stamp Duty in the American colonies in 1765. This event triggered the protests over "no taxation without representation". This historical accident not only has created vast economic damage, but contributed to the bloody American War of Independence. However, just like any accident, Stamp Duty should be corrected so that it does not continue to harm our economic prospects. Stamp Duty Reserve Tax is a tax not on bankers, but on savers and pushes up the cost of financing for companies. In fact, SDRT is estimated to destroy 3.5% of the average Brits life savings while pushing up the cost of capital for companies by 4-12%. This drives investment down, with SDRT estimated to lower business investment by £6.4bn. Scrapping SDRT would cost only £3.8bn while putting £10.2bn back into the UK economy generating tax receipts of around £3.4bn. People say there are no "free breakfasts" in this world, yet scrapping SDRT is one of those rare free breakfasts which make us both richer and is self-financing.

Unsurprisingly, tax cuts are very easy to pass as they tend to only create winners not losers, so no one feels cheated. Sadly though, sometimes we must push through tax increases to generate money for our public services and to pay for our other tax cuts. Politicians often talk about cracking down on "tax avoidance" as a way to avoid these tax rises on everyone else, however, the most effective anti "tax avoidance" measure is largely ignored by governments, because it would raise taxes on ordinary small businesses across the country. No politician wants to be the one who hiked taxes on "white van man". However, SME tax avoidance & evasion (tax gap) loses the taxman around £26.5bn a year. Fortunately, if we choose to fight this battle, we do have one simple weapon to vastly increase the tax take for the taxman and make it harder for SMEs to avoid their taxes, changing the VAT threshold. Currently SMEs don't have to pay a penny in VAT until their revenues hit £85,000. This not only loses VAT revenue, but also enables SMEs to understate their income dramatically to the tax man. There is no rational reason to allow businesses with revenues of £30,000, never mind £80,000 to avoid paying VAT. Even worse, this artificial limit persuades legal businesses to stay small in order to never cross the £85,000 revenue threshold. Cutting this threshold would be pro-growth, anti-tax avoidance and a significant revenue raiser. I had hoped that Phillip Hammond would have taken the chance to confront this absurdity of the tax system, yet unfortunately constrained by a weak government, he has been unable to take these political risks. If we are willing to take this political risk and cut the VAT threshold to just below the average wage at £26,000, we could raise £2bn of revenue instantly. Even more interestingly, the increased number and variety of VAT records would make it far easier for HMRC to identify SME's who are evading taxes by under-declaring their income.

The final and probably most contentious proposal is not strictly a tax change, but an agenda for radical transparency. We will never win the battle against tax evasion, until we truly know how much people are earning and can accurately estimate the tax they should be paying. Unfortunately, this will require us to follow the lead of the Norwegians and abandon a little of our privacy. Every single person's tax bill across the UK should be published, so that anyone can check their neighbours declared earnings to the tax man to see if they are the same as the way they live or if they are cheating everybody else by under-declaring their income. This will be uncomfortable for many, but if you truly want to make sure everyone pays their fair share of tax, it must be done. Based on Norway's experience, this simple change could raise significant tax revenue. No one said getting people to pay their taxes was a walk in the park.

Leaving the EU, we could also take aim at the tax havens within Europe's borders, which are shielded by the European Commission and join forces with Japan and the United States in fighting against EU shielded tax evasion and avoidance. Released from the constraints of membership, we can blacklist "dodgy" jurisdictions such as Malta and Luxembourg, shutting them out from UK capital markets. We will no longer be blocked by Jean Claude Juncker, current EU President and former Prime Minister of Luxembourg, from cracking down on the tax avoidance capital of Europe, Luxembourg.

The measures above are just a few of the changes which could propel the UK onto a new growth trajectory and build an economy that works for everyone. We will need to make hard decisions to get there and there will be pain. But step by step we can build a greater Britain.

CHAPTER 11: WELCOME TO THE AGE OF INNOVATION

Ronald Reagan once said that "The nine most terrifying words in the English language are: I'm from the government and I'm here to help." No place has this saying been truer than in the regulation of the industries of the future. The reality is that eurocrats have no idea about the structural reality of these advanced industries and completely fail to comprehend the damage that their uninformed regulations are doing to innovation across the continent. Well intentioned policy makers in Brussels have supressed innovation through regulatory control and will soon devastate the remaining pockets of technological innovation with misguided directives such as the GDPR (General Data Protection Regulation).

Now this may seem dull and technocratic, especially after battling through tax reform in the prior chapter, yet escaping the EU's regulatory chokehold will be one of the most stimulating benefits for the whole UK of leaving the EU. In layman's terms, the EU's regulatory policies require all European customer data to remain within the EU, unless an agreement is signed for this data to leave the country. This means that without hopping through your regulatory hurdles you won't be able to use your data stored on European web infrastructure to access non-EU sites. Small firms without the legal heft to organise these agreements will never be able to provide their services to EU customers. Even more worryingly the GDPR in particular requires that every firm have a dedicated data protection officer and processes to contact the EU authorities and mitigate a leak within 72 hours. This means that every small business must design systems from scratch to isolate every customer opinion survey, sales record, complaint & resolution detail and be able to identify and delete it with ease. Frankly, this is completely infeasible for many businesses, where customer data is only a small subsection of the overall business. Business will either ignore this rule or be crippled by it. The problem is that regulations for businesses are identical to incredibly regressive taxes, except that they fail to collect any tax revenue for the government and just destroy the wealth of these SMEs by wasting businesses so much time.

The EU's regulatory missteps are not just limited to the flawed regulatory climate for technology firms, but also in the chemicals sector. REACH is a bureaucrat's wet dream. Every chemical transported within the EU must be recorded on a central database at every point of movement. Now while it is sensible to keep a track record of hazardous chemical movements to ensure they don't get into the wrong hands, it is ludicrous to suggest that it is sensible to record the movements of every single chemical compound. Only 19% of chemical movement recorded by the REACH system is of severely hazardous chemicals (SHCs), and by removing less and non-dangerous chemicals from this centralised government control, we could reduce the regulatory burden of this system by 81%, while doing nothing to endanger the safety of Europeans.

Fundamentally, this has been the flaw in the EU's approach to regulation. By assuming that everything needs to be regulated until proven otherwise, it has stifled innovation and left the EU as a technology laggard compared to the other developed nations from Canada to Japan. Despite throwing billions of pounds into blue sky research, companies across the EU have struggled to commercialise this research and to enable these innovations to truly transform the global economy. Instead we have relied on importing vast technological advances from overseas to propel us forward. This does not mean that within the EU we have failed to come up with any significant innovations, however we have vastly underperformed our potential considering the vast supply of skilled researchers and capital available. Just think why, within the EU we have no technological superpower to contest with Facebook, Amazon or Google in the US or companies like Tencent in China. All this even though the EU is the second largest economic area on earth, narrowly behind the US.

So how might the UK look post-Brexit, as a home for high technology companies and advanced research and development? Well the UK has the best research universities in the world, with ground breaking blue-sky research being done up and down the length of the country with an extraordinary concentration of research facilities within the golden triangle of London, Cambridge and Oxford. However, the impressive thing about UK R&D is how widespread the research expertise is. Whether in sports science around Nottingham, driven by the competitive race between Loughborough and the University of Nottingham or in game design around Glasgow, the UK R&D scene is dynamic and strong.

The UK is almost unique in a European context by having an R&D scene dominated by private sector financing. This means that although the UK spends a smaller share of GDP on R&D than France, the UK is the leader in new technologies and produces almost 50% more patents per head of population. However, we can do so much better.

Developing the University-Industrial Complex

Some of the greatest advancements in technology we have made as a human species have been down to the military industrial complex. Without high levels of western military spending, we would never have created GPS, the jet engine or the internet. However, since the decline in military equipment spending over the last few decades, it has fallen to the private sector to pick up the slack and propel research and development forwards. Sadly though, despite the vibrancy and creativity of the private sector in the UK, we have not been able to propel ourselves forward as a research and development superpower. While the military industrial complex in Israel, has continued to produce ground breaking technologies and built an incredible entrepreneurial scene. Nonetheless I believe the age of military industrial complex driven growth is coming to an end and we are heading slowly into an increasingly demilitarised world, for which we should be very grateful. In this new era, it is vital that we develop a new growth pole to propel our technological advances forward and I propose that this growth pole shall be the university-industrial complex.

The UK has some of the best universities in the world, yet outside of Imperial College London and a couple of other world leading institutions, we lack the focused technical universities to contend with MIT, Caltech and the Indian Institutes of Technology. We need research universities which cater for the needs of the industries of tomorrow, building vast research centres where we begin to develop the technologies which will transform the world we live in. However, most importantly this cannot be the government picking winners and distorting the economic landscape with their own populist preferences.

As such I suggest the new age should be built on university industrial partnerships, where large firms and universities co launch specialised research cells within universities. Already many firms sponsor PhD students to embark on research which will be useful for the private firms, however, the government does little to nothing to support the financing of this research. Instead we should build a model of co-financing research PhDs across the country, where the government pays 50% of the cost of every PhD support program. Overnight this could double the number of PhD students producing research of genuine economic need and attract the brightest and best academics from all over the world. This simple reform could do wonders at propelling investment into ground breaking research and give British firms a leg up in their race for technological supremacy.

However, expanding the PhD research network is only the first step in crafting a new high-tech Britain. The second and much trickier stage is ensuring that these highly educated and specialised researchers deploy their skills in UK R&D rather than disappearing off overseas. The first step is to guarantee every PhD educated individual who has passed through the co-financing program the right to work in the UK for 2 years and secondly to require all PhDs who emigrate straight after graduation to pay back the cost of the PhD to the UK government over 2 years. These 2 simple measures should ensure that the UK trained talent does not leave straight after completing their doctorates.

Next, we need to deepen the research presence of the science parks dotted across the country. These already established research centres built around university cities have incubated some of the most valuable companies created in the UK in the last couple of decades, from Autonomy to ARM. With a new surge of research talent, there initially may be insufficient research projects that corporates will be able and willing to finance to employ all this new research talent. The government could step in at this point by financing "moonshot" research projects for advances which will have massive social benefits, but limited private benefit. This could include pumping money into financing Educational Artificial Intelligence to revolutionise our primary education system, where the brightest and best look into how to implement AI techniques in educational applications to deliver low cost learning for children across the world. The government could also seek to finance research projects into government service delivery, to test alternative methods of public transit or police monitoring. These research projects need not be expensive, and gradually the UK government can pull back its financing role, as Corporates and venture capitalists fill the breach and inject capital into the research industry.

This final wave of private sector driven innovation will only flourish if our financial services industry starts delivering capital to UK high growth companies. We already have the largest venture capital industry in Europe to build on, yet our venture capital sector is a mere minnow in comparison to the structure built up in Silicon Valley. Although it is true that as a country we are far more dependent on growth in London for our prosperity than we should be, the venture capital boom will need to start in London with investors pouring capital into the Golden Triangle between Oxford, Cambridge and London. This area has the highest density of skilled workers of anywhere in the world, as well as access to the world's leading financial centre. In fact, the Golden Triangle lacks only one key thing. An entrepreneurial mindset. However fantastic Oxbridge may be at producing the brightest and most capable workers, it fails to produce entrepreneurs & risk takers. The same issue exists in a lesser form across almost all British universities, in comparison to the entrepreneurial focus of the US university system. Fortunately, there are a couple of lessons we can steal from the Americans to foster this entrepreneurial ecosystem, and it needn't be expensive.

"Entrepreneurship, entrepreneurship, entrepreneurship. It drives everything: Job creation, poverty alleviation, innovation." – Elliott Bisnow

Universities in the US are the incubation engines of entrepreneurship, both financing and nourishing "want to be entrepreneurs" straight out of graduation. Encouraging students to take risks in the first few years of graduating, because if they fail they can always start into regular graduate life a couple of years late. Over in the US, entrepreneurship is not seen as the privilege of the rich, unlike in the UK where 50% of business ideas are financed from personal wealth, family and friends. Incubators could break this link between family wealth and entrepreneurship. These incubators also allow US universities to share in the success of their alumni, as the profits of successful investments are poured back into the universities. This would enable UK universities to gradually build up endowments and invest more into education without the government or students paying a penny more. Investing £680mn a year could enable each university to establish an incubator for themselves, financing start-ups for 13,500 graduating students every year. This cash injection over a 10-year period should be enough to permanently seed these incubator schemes and enable these universities to develop their own entrepreneurial ecosystems. Some will fail after government financing is withdrawn, however those successful incubator schemes, together with the PhD co-financing initiative and the "moonshot" plan, will become the foundations of a new entrepreneurial Britain.

CHAPTER 12: AGRICULTURAL AWAKENING

No sector will see more revolutionarily change by leaving the EU than agriculture. Our agricultural sector has grown fat and slow on EU subsidies; since 1991, productivity in agriculture has only grown by 0.4% a year, while the US and New Zealand outside of the EU have seen agricultural productivity grow by around 1.5% a year. The terrible thing about subsidies is that they make farmers distort their growing decisions and force them to farm the most subsidised crop instead of picking the best crop for the soil they have. In 2015, the EU wasted €58bn of taxpayers' money distorting the growing decisions of European farmers. It doesn't even lead to cheaper foodstuffs for ordinary European citizens, in fact leaving the CAP should lower the cost of food and drinks by 15% across the UK.

The Common Agricultural Policy and the combination of tariffs and subsidies have distorted and damaged the agricultural sector inside and outside the EU for too long. Yet, as discussed in chapter 4, we cannot let our post-Brexit policies get hijacked by the agricultural lobby. We should open our agricultural markets to all foreign competition with no tariffs or quotas on agricultural foodstuffs. This will hurt UK farming initially and there will be nasty scenes as inefficient farms close and dairy herd numbers plummet. However, sometimes we have to pass through pain to cure ourselves of our addictions. In this case, curing the farming communities' addiction to subsidies and protection. This is not an attack on the "green and pleasant land" of our islands or a threat to the environmental progress we have made in forests, rivers and the like; it is a restructuring to benefit the ordinary taxpayer.

Before you listen to the National Farmers Union howl in outrage that subsidy free agriculture is not possible, that this is madness and that there is no way that such a policy could ever be introduced successfully; let me remind you that this has been implemented before in a country far from our shores. New Zealand introduced just this policy 30 years ago and the results were nothing short of magical, after 2-3 years of agricultural contraction and pain, the agricultural sector rebounded ferociously, setting off 2 decades of productivity growth, which has left New Zealand with one of the most advanced agricultural sectors in the world!

The productivity revolution need not just be limited to tariff and subsidy reform. The fantastic thing about leaving the EU is that we can open agriculture up to the wonders of modern science. One technology currently banned in the EU boosts soy bean crop yields by 21%, while having no notable damaging effects to crop nutrition or the surrounding environment. MON 87769 x MON 89788, the banned GM strand of soy bean, has lowered the cost of soy globally, lowering the cost of both soy and all the meat products reared on soy. Beyond soy, the potential for GM crops in the UK is gargantuan. With some of the most advanced bio-engineering and genetics departments in the world located around London, Cambridge and Oxford we have the potential to become a world leader in field trials of GM crops. We will never be an agricultural superpower, we simply don't have enough land for that. Yet we do have some of the brightest scientists on Earth and with a simple regulatory change, their lab tests could be rolled out for testing by British farmers across the country.

Agricultural technology and innovation represents a frontier that we have barely addressed due to the stifling regulatory climate around food and drink in the EU. Wacky ideas, such as insect farms as a good source for protein to fight malnourishment is currently banned within the EU, despite there being no adverse threats to human health from consuming insects. This may seem niche and irrelevant, but if you compare testing insect based food products against Quorn, an artificial fungi grown in vats, it doesn't seem to be that bonkers. These small trials and tests are the baby steps which gradually transform the global agricultural industry.

Exploiting our vibrant biological research scene will be beneficial for farmers and allow them to be compensated for some of the financial pain of the repeal and abandonment of subsidies. Test fields for GM crops and other scientific research crops can generate up to 200% higher income for farmers, than regular crop farming.

Reforesting Britain

Nonetheless, in the short run farmers will suffer from their exposure to international competition. It would be unfair to not try and alleviate some of this pain that will be inflicted on farmers. One way in which we can insulate farmers from significant deteriorations in quality of living, is to restructure their role in Britain to be part farmer and part guardian of nature. Sadly, during the 18th century we devastated our natural landscape, felling forests to build hundreds upon thousands of military and commercial ships. We can undo the damage we have inflicted upon this country by continuing to pay farmers to reforest their least productive agricultural land. By directing small land improvement payments to farmers, we can ensure that our children and grandchildren grow up in a greener, more beautiful Britain than we ever managed to attain. The growth of forests can also help create new jobs in the eco-tourism sector, as the United Kingdom begins to exploit not just its historic assets but it's natural assets too. Imagine for a minute being able to enjoy with your 7-8-year-old children an interactive Robin Hood adventure in Nottingham forest or the mythology of Merlin in the forests of South Wales.

The Humanitarian Case

If none of the previous ideas have swayed your views on the Common Agricultural Policy, please think carefully about the humanitarian vision of Brexit.

Leaving the EU and abandoning the Common Agricultural Policy is not just a matter of economic logic, but also a matter of humanitarianism. One of the most damaging effects of the Common Agricultural Policy has been the economic damage inflicted upon Sub-Saharan Africa. By taxing heavily & in some cases banning the core export of less developed countries across Africa, we have: driven investment away from the African agricultural sector, weakened farmers income and trapped millions in poverty. It would be misleading if I said that the UK, alone, could transform the whole continent. We are only 65 million people out of a market of 500 million. However, by leaving the CAP we would boost the opportunities of those outside of fortress Europe and give a little income boost to farmers across Sub-Saharan Africa. By leaving CAP & maintaining our aid donations, we will be the humanitarian superpower of the world.

CHAPTER 13: ANTIBUREAUCRATIC PLANNING

Since the 1980's there has been a surge in economic productivity across manufacturing and services alike, following the liberalisation of product and services markets. In stark contrast, productivity in both construction and agriculture has been far weaker over the last three decades, held back by excessive regulation and protectionism respectively. Excessive planning restrictions have led to a chronic shortage of housing in the UK, pushing up rents and house prices relentlessly. As discussed in the prior chapter, generous subsidies have distracted farmers from improving agricultural productivity, and have instead diverted their focus onto exploiting Common Agricultural Policy (CAP) subsidies, which makes up 38% of UK farm income. We must relax excessive planning regulations to allow the construction industry to finally blossom and to wean the farming industry off of its subsidy addiction.

Subsidy reform is conceptually simple, however without a well-planned policy program for the transitional pain, this will be impossible to achieve without causing excessive hardship to the farming community. Correspondingly, deregulation of planning permission needs to be carefully designed so that we do not ruin the "Areas of Outstanding Natural Beauty" and vital wildlife reserves, which preserve the special natural diversity we have in this country. These two policy objectives may initially seem incompatible, yet farmers have one simple asset, which could help solve this dual problem: farmland.

69% of the UK is farmland — wide open spaces dedicated to the growing of crops and rearing of livestock for the UK and global market. It is dominated by monoculture and has severely limited biodiversity. So what if we allowed developers to build on this monoculture "greenbelt" land and allow farmers to cover the cost of the subsidy cuts with profits from small land sales to developers? If just 1% of UK land was converted from agricultural to residential land, we could build 12.1mn new homes (at the average UK density of 48 homes per hectare)[9], the relentless increase in rents and house prices could be halted, and we could begin to build the houses people actually want to live in.

Let us empower farmers to build these houses. We can allocate permits to farmers to convert a small share of their agricultural land into residential land, compensating them for their subsidy losses. These permits should be transferrable so that the farmer in the unpopulated Scottish Highlands can sell his Tradeable Planning Permits to a developer occupying land in the under-housed south east. This will ensure that houses are built where there is the highest demand for them; it will also maximise the farmers' incomes. Providing 11,000 TPPs a year to farmers should raise around £3.6bn a year — due to the strong price growth in developable land (see below) — enough to cover the loss of all CAP subsidies (whose abolition would save the UK government £3bn).

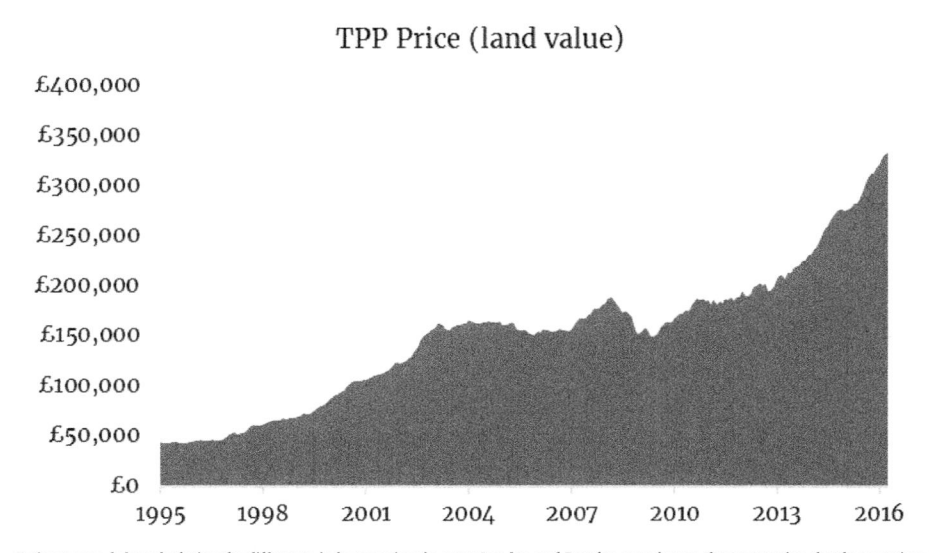

TPP Price (land value)

Estimates made by calculating the difference in house prices in outer London and Burnley, running on the assumption that house prices in Burnley are approximately equal to structure cost, while London prices reflect structure cost + land cost.

There will be protests, objections and legal challenges, as NIMBYs and environmentalists decry the destruction of "greenbelt" land, even if in reality it is dull monoculture land. They will moan about "profiteering" developers earning millions from the destruction of our natural landscape. Therefore, it is vital we compensate the "losers" from this decision through council tax cuts, investments in local infrastructure and investments in nature reserves. So we need to design a system which raises the revenue to at least cover the cost of compensating the NIMBYs and environmentalists, while further encouraging construction in the areas people want to live.

This revenue could easily be raised by the government selling additional TPPs to developers looking to convert agricultural to residential land. Selling 160,000 TPPs a year would raise approximately £53bn a year in direct revenue and far more in increased tax take from the increased economic activity. This would be enough to finance the abolition of air passenger duty, compensate NIMBYs, raise the national insurance threshold to £12,500 (aligning it with income tax cuts), 2 more Crossrail lines, build a new 4 runway Thames Estuary airport and a new underground system for Birmingham, Leeds and Manchester by 2025.

The greatest benefit of these reforms and the construction boom that would follow may be to stabilise rents. According to the Shelter report "Building the Homes We Need", raising housebuilding levels to around 250,000 homes a year should lead to price stabilization[6], putting an end to inflation busting house price and rental increases. Slower house price and rental increases near to economic hubs in Cambridge, London, Leeds or Manchester will encourage internal migration to these booming areas. Finally, there would be a boost to UK productivity, as workers shift from low wage periphery areas to these high wage centres of economic growth. This construction program could become a pillar of the new industrial strategy to boost productivity and allow the government to finally deliver housing that people want to live in.

Why Can't We Just Build on Brownfield?

So, if we need more housing, why can't we just build on Brownfield land? That neglected industrial wasteland, blighting the inner parts of our cities and now just stands there derelict. The reality is we already do, yet Brownfield land suitable for housing only makes up 0.1% of UK land.[9] Even if every inch of Brownfield land was used for additional housing, we could only build 1.5mn new homes in total. In fact, the previous Labour government's target of using 60% of brownfield land for construction "encouraged houses with large gardens" to be "replaced with denser housing or blocks of flats", as private gardens were defined as brownfield sites.[9] Why not be more imaginative with this brownfield land and focus on beautifying the centres of our towns? Instead of building at a high cost on brownfield sites, brownfield sites could be reclaimed for central parks and green spaces in the centre of our cities.

Size (hectares)

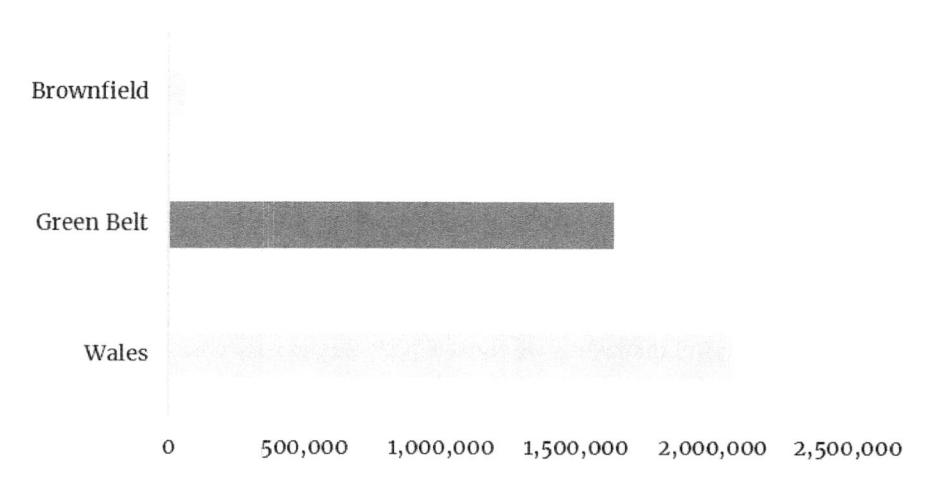

Brownfield	(minimal)
Green Belt	~2,200,000
Wales	(minimal)

0   500,000   1,000,000   1,500,000   2,000,000   2,500,000

As can be seen above, the reality is that we have vast amounts of bland monoculture agricultural land in the Green Belt in England, almost as much as the whole of Wales. While brownfield land will never be enough to cover our housing need, a small share of agricultural land in the Green Belt could easily provide enough land for all our housing needs without losing any Areas of Outstanding Natural Beauty.

Paying Off Opponents?

It can be concluded that farmers will be better off, housing will be more affordable, and the government could raise around £53bn from TPP sales. But these reforms could anger a vast number of homeowners on the border with the greenbelt, as well as anti-construction environmentalists. So how do we overcome this local resistance?

Earmarking £3.2bn of funds raised for council tax breaks in areas around development could grant 10 households around each new home a £2000 tax break and £1.8bn could be earmarked for reclaiming derelict land for public parks; wildlife reserves could appease the environmentalist objections. Even after these earmarks, the government would be left with around £46bn a year to spend on tax cuts, infrastructure improvements or paying government debt down.

Conclusion

The UK's economic potential has been limited by ludicrously tight planning laws, which have punished the young and poor by driving up residential rents; high commercial rents have rendered manufacturing in large parts of the country uncompetitive. For too long developers have exploited the planning system, making large windfall gains every time a development is approved. It is time that those windfall gains are shared among all taxpayers, not just the few developers with lawyers expensive enough to obtain planning permission.

Imagine a policy, which boosted economic growth, improved agricultural productivity, raised tens of billions in tax revenues, pushed down rents and left the country more beautiful than when we started. Isn't that exactly what a cash starved new One Nationist government should be looking for?

THE END: YOUR ROLE IN BUILDING A TRULY GREAT BRITAIN

I hope that you have enjoyed reading this book and didn't feel too trapped in the technicalities within it. I know that some of the concepts may have been pretty complex and my writing style is not the cleanest that you've probably read. Yet having reached the end of this book you have heard of many real opportunities which our country could seize, if only there was political appetite for it. At the moment, the news coverage and mission statements coming out of the UK government seem highly disappointing and somewhat depressing, however we can change this together and ensure that we create a Brexit which works for everyone.

Whether you agree or disagree with my conclusions, you all have a vision of what you want our country to be. So please, I implore you, write to your local MP, offer to campaign for movements to transform this country. Take the initiative and stand for your local authority. Stand for parliament even! We have been a sleeping nation, politically and socially, people have become disenfranchised and detached from the governments and policies which shape our lives. We have taken a backseat, while a small elite minority has captured government for their interests, and there is no one to blame but ourselves.

This revolution does not end at the ballot box. It is only the beginning. We must also recognise the extraordinary privilege in growing up in such prosperity, safe from war and disease. To paraphrase Spiderman, "with great privilege comes great responsibility". You all have a responsibility to change the world that we live in. Imagine for a minute if we all worked just 20 minutes longer every day, we would boost GDP by 5% and eliminate the deficit overnight. We could relax spending constraints on our public services and discard austerity to the dustbins of history. How much effort does it actually take to volunteer on one weekday evening? Finishing at

6:00 and driving down to your local football club to coach the kids and give them something to do rather than getting dragged into gangs.

The government may talk about wanting to foster a "Big Society", but the only way it will take hold is if we take responsibility for it. The difference is the individual. The norm should be to volunteer to build the collaborative society. Not to leave it to the exceptional man or women who takes that responsibility today. It is our duty to volunteer and give back to our community. I personally have been weak on this in recent times and have barely done any volunteer work in the past year, blaming my workload, lack of time – all rubbish excuses. Everyone has time to give back and do something for their community. Imagine if we lived in a world where "volunteering avoidance" became as hated as "tax avoidance". If we, as the people of Britain, want to build this better world, the first step is to take responsibility for ourselves, and ask ourselves what can we do in our lives to improve the lives of others around us?

This may seem soft and flaky to many of you. But it isn't. A country is only as great as the people who make it and without a transformation in the mindset of Brits, we can never truly transform Britain. So step into the world and sign up to your local volunteering network. Commit yourself to improving the lives of others and you can build a Greater Britain. You can be the foot soldiers of this revolution, you can change this world.

ECONOMIC PROJECTIONS & THEORY

Throughout this book, many complex themes and solutions were introduced, however they were not discussed in deep detail, unfortunately this would have required a book longer than The Iliad to truly explain and challenge each policy provision. However, I recognise that many readers may want to read more deeply into particular policies touched upon here. Therefore, to aid the reader, I have constructed a reading list of interesting background literature on each key topic touched upon, at the end of this book. For those of you who want a slightly easier read, and may not have the deep economic interest to investigate every policy, please see below the estimated economic and financial impact of each policy proposal mentioned in these chapters. All GDP effects ignore the fiscal multiplier effect of tax cuts or spending increases, as all tax cuts/spending increases will be offset by tax increases/spending cuts elsewhere. All GDP changes due to structural improvements will not generate a fiscal change in each individual table, instead the aggregate fiscal change will be calculated at the end of this section. I.e. EU net payment reduction, shifting of tax burden from UK to foreign firms. For these GDP benefits are assumed to be only £1 for every £1 saved. In addition, all costs of infrastructure and capital investment deals are assumed to be spread out over 10 years, unless otherwise stated. I.e. a new airport costing £30bn to build, would be listed as having a fiscal change of -£3bn a year.

Chapter 1: Getting the Best Deal with the EU

Proposed Guarantees for UK Companies

Policy	Fiscal Change	GDP Effect	Benefit
Withdraw From EU, EEA and ECU	+£14.6bn	+£10.3bn	Liberation from single market regulations and net payments
Governments pays EU manufacturing tariffs	-£5.5bn	-£5.5bn	Offsets negative GDP effect of customs union tariffs

Policy	Fiscal Change	GDP Effect	Benefit
Match EU research spending	-£1.1bn	Neutral	Maintains research plans by UK science
Match EU regional aid spending	-£1bn	Neutral	Matches all other EU cash injections into UK except CAP

So overall, the cost of guaranteeing little to no damage from a hard Brexit would be around £7.6bn a year, £7bn less than our annual EU contributions of £14.6bn a year. Importantly £5.5bn of this would never need to be spent if we were to gain a Brexit deal with tariff free access to the EU.

Costs of "Singapore West" No Deal

Policy	Fiscal Change	GDP Effect	Benefit
5% Corporation Tax	-£35.0bn	+24.0bn	Mass corporate investment. HQ shifts from EU to UK. 1.2% GDP increase (from OECD/Irish Gov)
Abolishing Air Passenger Duty	-£3.2bn	+16.0bn	Steal air traffic from European hubs and airports.
Skilled worker visas	£0bn	Neutral	Skilled labour supply for all UK industries, offsetting negative of EU migration controls

Singapore West would be an expensive gambit and may lead to negative foreign policy implications with the EU. Maximum cost is assumed with no increase in business investment or hiring by firms. Naturally such an aggressive set of tax cuts would increase economic activity. However, I have chosen to display the worst-case scenario. The £38.2bn tax cut, may seem severe, yet in reality we would see a surge in income tax, VAT and other tax receipts. For all of the tax and spending changes highlighted in the other chapters, I have ignored the multiplier effect on tax revenues. This is simply because the overall proposals in this book will be fiscally neutral and as such, any tax cuts or spending increases will be offset by tax increases or spending cuts elsewhere. We should therefore be able to ignore the net demand effects for the sake of this analysis.

Background Readings

Fullfact. 2017. Everything you might want to know about the UK's trade with the EU
Frenk, C., Hunt, T., Partridge, L., Thornton, J. and Wyatt, T. 2016. UK research and the European Union: The role of the EU in funding UK research.
Soubry, A. 2016. EU Grants and Loans: Written question – 33071.
Irish Department of Finance. 2014. Economic impact assessment of Ireland's corporation tax policy
PWC. 2013. The economic impact of Air Passenger Duty.

Chapter 2: Building the Great Meritocracy

Proposed Educational Programs

Policy	Fiscal Change	GDP Effect	Benefit
Language/Programming immersion year	-£1.6bn	-£0.8bn	Programming and language skills for all new students
Education Vouchers	Neutral	Neutral	Edtech innovation
£250 retraining vouchers	-£1.2bn	Neutral	Reskilling of those left behind by globalisation

For the costing I have assumed that 50% of eligible students choose to take the language/programming immersion year. The retraining voucher scheme is assumed to initially only have a take up of 10% of adults (18-65), as most people see little need in additional educational training.

Background Readings

Fullfact. 2012. Were a quarter of prisoners in care as children?
Bingham, J. 2014. How private schooling is deciding the millionaires of tomorrow.
Hall, J. 2011. Millionaires more likely to have gone to state school.
Clarke, A. 2012. Schools, pupils, and their characteristics.

Chapter 3: Forging an Open Trading World

Theory of specialisation

Humanity has become rich on the basis that we have specialised our job focus and social roles on a skill set that we are good at. This allows us to become experts in our particular niche rather than being "jack of all trades, but master of none". This specialisation and division of tasks into specialised functions, enables us to be far more productive as a group than we could ever be as individuals. For instance in a Toyota car manufacturing plant, every person has their own specialised role on the production line and collectively they produce more cars than they ever could without the production line. This has pushed down the cost of goods, boosted our productivity and driven earnings growth.

Theory of comparative advantage

The theory of comparative advantage is remarkably simple. Countries can get rich from trade in a similar way to people through specialisation. Even though a US worker can produce more toys with American technology than his counterpart in Cambodia. China and Cambodia export toys to the US. This is because the US worker is good at making toys, but better at IT services. Therefore, Cambodia specialises in low skilled manufacturing, using the cheap plentiful Cambodian labour, while the US exports back packages of Microsoft office and new medical devices. This trade allows both the US and Cambodia to specialise at what they are best at and therefore makes both countries richer.

For instance, a US worker working 1 day can make 200 toys or 10 medical devices and a Cambodian worker working 1 day can make 100 toys or 1 medical device. Let's say there are 10 Cambodian workers and Cambodia needs 10 medical devices a day and at the same time there are 3 US workers and the US needs 20 medical devices a day. Without trade Cambodia would use all it's labour to make medical devices and have no toys. At the same time 2 US workers would make medical devices and the remaining US worker would only be making 200 toys. If instead they started trading, the 3 US workers could all make medical devices and the Cambodians could make toys. The 3 US workers would make 30 medical devices, enough for the US and Cambodia and the Cambodians would make 1000 toys. So before trade the US and Cambodia only made 200 toys and 30 medical devices. Now with trade the US and Cambodia make 1000 toys and 30 medical devices. In other words, due to comparative advantage and trade we are 800 toys richer.

Background Readings

Smith, P. 2016. A Short History of How Britain Feeds Itself.
Shankar, A., Greer, A., Newman, H., Booth, S. and Scarpetta, V. 2017. Global Britain: Priorities for trade beyond the EU

Shankar, A., Booth, S. and Scarpetta, V. 2017. Nothing to declare: A plan for UK-EU trade outside the Customs Union.
Smith, A. and McCulloch, J.R. 1838. An Inquiry into the Nature and Causes of the Wealth of Nations. A. and C. Black and W. Tait.
Ricardo, D., 2005. The Principles of Political Economy and Taxation. In Readings In The Economics Of The Division Of Labor: The Classical Tradition (pp. 127-130).

Chapter 4: Crushing Crony Capitalism

Background Reading

Niemietz, K. 2013. Abolish the CAP, let food prices tumble.
Rutter, T and Gil, N. 2014. Which private companies get the most UK government money?
Koumenta, M., Humphris, A., Kleiner, M. and Pagliero, M. 2014. Occupational Regulation in the EU and UK: Prevalence and Labour Market Impacts.

Chapter 5: Building Bridges to a Brighter Future

Proposed Educational Programs

Policy	Fiscal Change	GDP Effect	Benefit
Upgrade 50% C, D & U road network	-£13.0bn	+£6.5bn	Self-driving cars Congestion elimination
Cycle & pedestrian paths on roads (50%)	-£4.1bn	Neutral	Cyclists protected and have no congestion effects
500,000 electric charger stations	-£1.5bn	Neutral	Self-driving cars Emissions mitigation
Rail Expansion	-£8bn	+£4bn	Transit time reduction

Road upgrades assume 50% of 196,306 miles of C, D & U network roads are transformed into new 2-4 lane roads on a road cost of £1.3mn per mile. Cycle path construction assumes a construction cost of £200,000 per mile. Costs for both are spread over 10 years of construction. In contrast the 500,000 charger stations are to be installed within 5 years. Assumed GDP effect of congestion reductions as 50% of spending.

Cost Benefit Analysis

Cost benefit analysis relies on the idea that infrastructure projects and other forms of government capital spending can have their benefits quantified and isolated. For instance, building a bridge across a river may save commuters 5 minutes a day once opened. Under cost benefit analysis governments attempt to put a monetary price on the value of the average commuter's minute. The value of minutes saved is then compared to the cost of building the bridge and if the value is higher than the cost the bridge project goes ahead. One core problem with cost benefit analysis is it tends to be very static, so a bridge to a new city being built would be recorded as having limited to no benefit now, however in reality it will have massive benefits once the city was built.

Dynamic Modelling

The solution to the conundrum of static cost benefit analysis is called dynamic modelling. Dynamic modelling attempts to simulate the effect of a policy, given that another policy will be introduced. This means that under this modelling framework, policy makers include the effect of changing circumstances in their decision making. For instance, if self-driving cars are about to be legalised, dynamic modelling would adjust the expected return of installing electric charge points. Unfortunately, dynamic models can be manipulated by academics to prove any point they want to as they often really on multiple assumptions which feedback on each other. Nonetheless dynamic modelling offers a handy adjustment for flawed static cost benefit analysis.

Background Reading

Fullfact. 2017. House building in England.
Parveen, N. 2017. More than half UK investment in transport is in London, says study.
BBA. 2015. Financing the UK's infrastructure needs.
Leduc, S. and Wilson, D. 2012. Highway Grants: Roads to Prosperity?

Chapter 7: Immigration, Integration and Innovation

Revenue from New Migration Visa System (after 6 years)

Policy	Fiscal Change	GDP Effect	Benefit
£5,000 working visas	+£10.2bn	+£10.2bn	Reduction in low skilled migration, increase in high skilled migration
£10,000 entrepreneur visas	+£3.0bn	+£3.0bn	Increase in number of start-ups
English language course	-£0.3bn	Neutral	Self-driving cars Emissions mitigation

Assuming an average cost of English language lessons at £3000 with 25% uptake, gross migration levels averaging 400,000 people. Assuming the average migrant receives citizenship after 6 years. If migrant levels are different, then for every 1,000 extra migrants per year we will raise around £29mn after English language course costs.

Background Reading

Natcen. 2013. British Social Attitudes Report.
Inglehart, R. and Norris, P. 2016. Trump, Brexit, and the rise of populism: Economic have-nots and cultural backlash.

Chapter 8: Green, Lean & Mean Manufacturing

Revenue from Green & Hi-Tech Schemes (Long run)

Policy	Fiscal Change	GDP Effect	Benefit
Carbon Added Tax revenue	+£44bn	Neutral	Rejuvenation of the UK manufacturing sector Reduction in carbon emission
Elimination of hi-tech tariffs	-£0.7bn	Neutral	Access to the latest technology
Investment expensing	Neutral	Neutral	Self-driving cars Emissions mitigation

Increasing tax revenue from the CAT tax will shift the tax burden onto polluting foreign manufacturers, allowing environmentally friendly UK manufacturers to regain competitiveness. Tax revenue can be used to lower other UK taxes.

Externalities

Externalities are costs or benefits imposed on others who do not take part in the economic transaction, which creates these externalities. For instance, if I buy cigarettes and smoke them in my car with a passenger, the passenger didn't gain anything from selling me the cigarettes, but he suffered the cigarette smoke and the risk of cancer. The cigarette smoke is the externality in this case. Environmental damage, including greenhouse gas emissions are also a classic example of where others suffer because of the private decision of someone to buy petrol to fill up their car. These externalities hurt everybody and so according to theory, we could all be better off if the products which create these externalities were taxed.

Background Reading

Eurostat. 2016. Greenhouse gas emissions.
Beales, R. 2017. UK emission targets.
Pigou, A.C., 1912. Wealth and welfare. Macmillan and Company, limited.
Elliott, J., Foster, I., Kortum, S., Munson, T., Cervantes, F.P. and Weisbach, D., 2010. Trade and carbon taxes. The American Economic Review, 100(2), pp.465-469.
Ismer, R. and Neuhoff, K., 2007. Border tax adjustment: a feasible way to support stringent emission trading. European Journal of Law and Economics, 24(2), pp.137-164.

Chapter 9: Financial Revolution

Proposed Reforms

Policy	Fiscal Change	GDP Effect	Benefit
Scrap CRD IV	Neutral	+£4.6bn	Reduce the cost of borrowing for UK firms
Scrap AIFMD	Neutral	+£1.5bn	Increase pension fund returns and savings returns
Introduce RIFs	Neutral	+£6.0bn	Increased investment in illiquid assets and higher returns for retail investors
Replace Bank Levy with Capital Inadequacy Levy	Neutral	Neutral	Increase financial systematic security by punishing banks who have low capital levels

Underlying Theory

In this chapter, we covered a wide range of financial concepts, some of which were simple, yet many which were remarkably complex. I will therefore explain 3 core theoretical concepts, around which the Brexit literature largely depends:

1. Illiquidity Premium
2. Debt-Capital Efficiency: The Corporate Tax Shield
3. Allocative efficiency

Illiquidity Premium

A liquidity premium is the fact that investors need to have a higher expected return if they own something which is illiquid or hard to sell. This happens because no investor would invest in an asset where he/she expected to make the same amount of money as another investment, if the 1st investment was hard to sell. There is a risk with an illiquid asset that you won't be able to sell it, because of this, illiquid assets trade at a discounted price in comparison to liquid assets and therefore have a higher expected return.

Debt-Capital Efficiency: The Corporate Tax Shield

Companies take on debt, not because they can't raise equity, but because it has a tax shielding benefit. Company profits must pay corporation tax at a company levels before being paid out to investors as dividends. These dividends will face the investors personal income taxes when paid out. In contrast, if a company borrow money from a shareholder and pays interest on that loan, then any profits paid out as interest can be paid out without paying any corporation tax, lowering their corporation tax bill. So, the investor only pays income tax on the loan income. This means that investors, who want to put money in their company, lend money to their company instead of investing it into equity, so that they can lower their tax bill.

Allocative Efficiency

Allocative efficiency is a slightly more complex concept. Allocative efficiency is the either that society can be richer without any improvement in productivity or technological advance. Instead we can become richer by spending our money on the right things. In investments, this could be as simple as making sure enough money is invested in high returning, high risk assets. Under a functioning free market, this should happen automatically, however regulation can stop people from allocating their investments efficiently and leave society poorer.

Background Readings

Miller, H. 2017. What's been happening to corporation tax?
BBA. 2015. Banks pay additional £40 billion in taxes.
IMF 2016. Global Financial Stability Report.
Booth, S. and Scarpetta, V. 2017. How the UK's financial services sector can continue thriving after Brexit.
Bangs, R. 1941. Public and Private debt in the United States 1929-1940.
Chan, H.W. and Faff, R.W., 2005. Asset pricing and the illiquidity premium. Financial Review, 40(4), pp.429-458.

Chapter 10: True Tax Reform

Tax Changes

Policy	Fiscal Change	GDP Effect	Benefit
Introduce Border Adjustment Tax	+£7.2bn	+£23.6bn	Shift of burden to foreign firms with taxes levied on foreign exporters of £70bn
Scrap Corporate Interest Deduction	+£15.2bn	Neutral	Reduced leverage in corporations, so more financial stability
Stamp Duty abolition	-£12bn	+£10bn	Reduced deposits to buy houses More mobile labour market
VAT limit change	+£2bn	Neutral	Increased SME formalisation and reduction in black market

Background Readings

HMRC. 2016. Corporation Tax: tax deductibility of corporate interest expense.
Rolet, X. 2009. Stamp Duty – A UK Financial Transaction Tax.
Full Fact. 2016. Tax: evasion and avoidance in the UK.
FSB. 2017. Business Population Estimates for the UK and Regions in 2017.
Bowers, S. 2016. Experts dismiss HMRC's shrinking tax gap estimate.
HMRC. 2017. HMRC Annual Report and Accounts 2016-17 – Executive Summary.
Schneider, F., Raczkowski, K. and Mroz, B. 2015. Shadow economy and tax evasion in the EU.
Auerbach, A.J., Devereux, M.P., Keen, M. and Vella, J., 2017. Destination-Based Cash Flow Taxation.

Chapter 11: Welcome to the Age of Innovation

Innovation Spending

Policy	Fiscal Change	GDP Effect	Benefit
Co-Sponsor PhDs	-£0.6bn	Neutral	Doubling PhD students
Moonshot programs	-£1.2bn	Neutral	Ground breaking research
University incubators	-£0.7bn	Neutral	Entrepreneurial centres

Co-Sponsor of PhDs on basis of government covering living costs of £18,000 a year for PhDs and the corporate sponsor covering all others. Innovation spending on moonshot program, doubling current EU science spending in the UK.

Background Readings

Eurostat. 2017. Chemicals production and consumption statistics.
Jump, P. 2012. PhD completion rates.
Phillips, R.G., 2002. Technology business incubators: how effective as technology transfer mechanisms?. Technology in society, 24(3), pp.299-316.
Pena, I., 2002. Intellectual capital and business start-up success. Journal of intellectual capital, 3(2), pp.180-198.

Chapter 12: Agricultural Awakening

Agricultural Programs

Policy	Fiscal Change	GDP Effect	Benefit
Reforestation subsidy	-£0.3bn	Neutral	Reforestation of marginal crop land

Background Readings

Kaushish, R. 2015. UK agricultural productivity fails to keep pace with global trends.
Gosden, E. and Dakers, M. 2016. What would Brexit mean for farmers and the Common Agricultural Policy?
Hettinger, J. 2017. From yield protection to yield boosting: GMO crops of the future.
EC Health and Food Safety. 2017. GM Register.
Sandrey, R. and Reynolds, R., 1990. Farming without subsidies: New Zealand's recent experience. Ministry of Agriculture and Fisheries.

Chapter 13: Antibureaucratic Planning

Proposed Reforms

Policy	Fiscal Change	GDP Effect	Benefit
Tradable Planning Permit Sales	+£53bn	Neutral	Raise lots of revenue. Boost building rates
Council Tax Breaks	-£3.2bn	Neutral	Overcome resistance of NIMBYs. Share prosperity of projects
Derelict land conversion to parks	-£1.8bn	Neutral	Public parks for city dwellers. Wildlife reserves for biodiversity
New underground systems	-£11.1bn	+£5.5bn	Metro system for Leeds, Manchester and Birmingham
Thames Estuary Airport	-£4.8bn	+£2.4bn	Airport capacity for the future, not just today
2 more Crossrail lines	-£2.8bn	+£1.4bn	London underground system unblocked
Abolish Air Passenger Duty	-£3.2bn	+£16.0bn	Steal air traffic from European hubs and airports.
National Insurance threshold increase to £12,500	-£18.7bn	Neutral	Tax cut for all minimum wage earners across the country

Infrastructure spending spread out over 10 years. Annual cost one tenth of total infrastructure costs. For congestion combating infrastructure, a conservative 0.5 increase in annual GDP is assumed, ignoring demand effects.

Background Readings

Glaeser, E.L., 2012. Triumph of the city: How our greatest invention makes us richer, smarter, greener, healthier, and happier. Penguin.
Savills. 2015. Land values to increase in 2015.
HM Land Registry. 2016. UK House Price Index: data downloads April 2016.
Proeger, T., Meub, L. and Bizer, K. 2015. Tradable development right under uncertainty: An experimental approach.
Tenant Farmers Association. 2016. Post Brexit Replacement to the Common Agricultural Policy.
Crossrail. 2017. Crossrail in numbers.

Corlett, A. 2014. Making allowances: tax cuts for the squeezed middle.
Pope, T. and Waters, T. 2016. A survey of the UK tax system.
Fullfact. 2012. Is there enough brownfield land for 1.5 million?
CLG. 2012. National Planning Policy Framework Impact Assessment.
Fed Farm. 2005. Life after subsidies – the NZ experience.
Muller, N., Werner, P. and Kelcey, J. 2010. Urban Biodiversity and Design.
Matthews, A. 2016. The dependence of EU farm income on public support,

Overview

Chapter Totals

Policy	Fiscal Change	GDP Effect	Benefit
Getting the Best Deal with the EU	+£12.5bn	+£10.3bn	EU membership fee savings Escaping single market regulation
Building the Great Meritocracy	-£2.8bn	-£0.8bn	Social mobility gains Educational technology advance
Building Bridges to a Brighter Future	-£26.6bn	+£10.5bn	Infrastructure upgrade
Immigration, Integration and Innovation	+£12.9bn	+£13.2bn	Boosting skilled migration Cutting unskilled migration Reducing cultural division
Green, Lean & Mean Manufacturing	+£43.3bn	Neutral	Restoring UK manufacturing Reducing emission levels
Financial Revolution	Neutral	+£12.1bn	Increased pension size Reduced financial inequality
True Tax Reform	+£12.4bn	+£33.6bn	Reduced tax avoidance Strengthened exporters
Welcome to the Age of Innovation	-£2.5bn	Neutral	R&D spending increase Company creation rate increase
Agricultural Awakening	-£0.3bn	Neutral	Increased farming of efficient crops, not subsidised ones
Antibureaucratic Planning	+£7.4bn	+£25.3bn	Increase housebuilding Raise revenue for tax cuts

In addition, the increase in GDP of £104bn would generate tax revenues of around £35bn. Therefore, even with the surge of investment into infrastructure, the reforms and tax rises highlighted in this book would leave us with around £91bn to finance further spending increases or tax cuts. Now these increases would not occur overnight, as infrastructure investments and reforms take up to 10 years to bear fruit. Nonetheless this spare cash generated could finance increased deficit reduction, tax cuts or spending increases. With that in mind, please see below a list of potential spending increases or tax cuts which could be paid for using this spare cash.

Public Policy Shopping List

Policy	Fiscal Change	GDP Effect	Benefit
Give £350mn a week to the NHS	-£18.2bn	Neutral	Fill a funding gap in the NHS Finance investment in additional research
Scrap Tuition Fees and new grants	-£12.7bn	Neutral	Reduce student debt issue Fight intergenerational inequality
Free Prescriptions	-£0.5bn	Neutral	Middle class income boost
Build Heathrow and Gatwick	-£2.7bn	+£1.4bn	Infrastructure for the future Air traffic congestion relief
Scrap Business Rates	-£28.4bn	Neutral	Relief for businesses Price & Rent Increases
Scrap Council Tax	-£30.1bn	Neutral	Relief for homeowners Price & Rent increases
Cut VAT to 15%	-£30.6bn	Neutral	Airport capacity for the future, not just today
Cut top income tax rates to 20%	-£32.7bn	Neutral	Increased migration of high skilled workers Increased income to high paid
Scrap all tariffs	-£3.1bn	Neutral	Lower cost goods in UK Embrace of free trade
Eliminate the deficit	£18.2bn	Neutral	Fixing the roof while the sun is shining

Again, all infrastructure spending assumed to be spread out over 10 years.

Background Readings

Ryan, F. 2017. Labour's scrapping of tuition fees isn't the progressive measure it appears.
Black, L. 2014. Prescription costs and charges in the UK and Republic of Ireland.
Manning, A. 2015. Top rate of income tax
Thompson, D. 1938. The Beano 1st edition
^^^ Not really, but congratulations for getting to the end of the book! I hope you have enjoyed reading it, at least as much as I did writing this thing.

Book Title Copyright © 2017 by Louis Williams. All Rights Reserved.

All rights reserved. No part of this book may be reproduced in any form or by any electronic or mechanical means including information storage and retrieval systems, without permission in writing from the author. The only exception is by a reviewer, who may quote short excerpts in a review.

Cover designed by CTC

Louis Williams

First Printing: Dec 2017
CTC Publishing

Learn more about the Author

| LinkedIn | Instagram | About Me |

Printed in Great Britain
by Amazon